DOPAMINE DETOX

DOPAMINE DETOX

BIOHACKING YOUR WAY TO BETTER FOCUS, GREATER HAPPINESS, AND PEAK PERFORMANCE

NICK TRENTON

AMARYLLIS

An imprint of Manjul Publishing House

AMARYLLIS

An imprint of Manjul Publishing House Pvt. Ltd.
• C-16, Sector 3, Noida, Uttar Pradesh 201 301, India
Website: www.manjulindia.com

Registered Office:
• 2nd Floor, Usha Preet Complex, 42 Malviya Nagar,
Bhopal 462 003 – India

Distribution Centres
Ahmedabad, Bengaluru, Chennai, Hyderabad,
Kochi, Kolkata, Mumbai, Noida, Pune

Dopamine Detox – Biohacking Your Way to Better Focus, Greater Happiness, and Peak Performance by Nick Trenton

English rights arranged with PKCS Mind, Inc.
through TLL Literary Agency

This edition first published by
Manjul Publishing House Pvt. Ltd. copyright © 2025

This paperback edition first published in India in 2025
Fourth impression 2026

ISBN 978-93-5543-744-0

Printed and bound in India by Repro India Ltd.

Contents

PART 1

Dopamine and Your Brain

Every single person reading this book will share one thing in common: they inhabit biological bodies. But there is something else they may or may not possess, and that's the ability to think consciously about their physical well-being. This awareness allows them to take proactive steps to strategize and improve on their life, no matter what kind of body they're working with.

"Biohacking" is broadly defined as any attempt to improve, upgrade, or enhance the biological realities of human life. Originally, biohackers were renowned for DIY experiments with drugs, gene editing, or body modification techniques that fell far outside of conventional science and medicine. In time, however, ordinary people also acquired a taste for embracing their power to use science to improve on what nature endowed them with.

In the chapters that follow, we'll be exploring three key areas in which the art of "biohacking" has been practiced, and several everyday ways that you can use these principles to your own advantage. Thankfully, you don't need to go to extremes to make drastic changes to your longevity, mood, mental faculties, self-discipline, and overall vitality. Whether it's a good sleep schedule and the right supplements, or a completely rebooted dopamine system, we'll explore practical and proven techniques for making the best of your life, here and now.

If you could do one thing to improve your life drastically, what would it be?

There are countless books out there on self-discipline, productivity, self-esteem, purposeful living, emotional resilience, and more. But could there be something that underlies all these separate behaviors, attitudes, and mindsets? Well, yes. Maybe the secret ingredient for a life that is disciplined, focused, proactive, and balanced is simple: dopamine.

As neuroscientists gain a more sophisticated understanding of the physiological correlates of our mood, our cognition, and our behavior, it becomes clear that any serious change to our lifestyle must include a change to our biology. For a biohacker, the neurochemicals—hormones and electrical connections in the brain—are akin to the programming in a computer; if we can rewrite the code at the back end of our own biology, we can influence the programs we run.

Understanding the effects of dopamine on the human experience requires a bit of a perspective shift. Think of yourself as both the machine and the programmer—you are able to consciously control your own experience if you understand the rules of its operation. In layman's terms, the brain is a neurochemical machine that operates according to a variety of hormones and neurotransmitters, which can be thought of as chemical messengers or instructions for the body. In a literal way, they are the concrete expression of your reality. For example, every time you feel love, disappointment, fear, or frustration, there is a precise neurochemical state in your body associated with the experience. It follows then that if we can alter this state, we can work backward and engineer our experience from the bottom up. In fact, in all the chapters that follow, we will inevitably be working with our neurochemistry, in one way or another, consciously or unconsciously.

One of the primary neurochemicals that operate in the brain is dopamine, which is linked to pleasure, motivation, reward, and so much more. For a long time, dopamine was considered to be a "reward chemical". While this is not entirely untrue, we now know that it is more linked to the *anticipation* of reward and the search for more and better things than are available. Dopamine engages when we face a surprise—an unexpected pleasure that fills us with delight, which fills our brain with dopamine. Unexpected rewards provide us a lot of joy, while expected ones are subject to hedonic adaptation or the hedonic treadmill—i.e., things lose their novelty and shine and stop providing us the same feeling of reward (Lieberman & Long, 2018, *The Molecule of More*).

Imagine this: you discover a new restaurant. It opened near your workplace, and you look forward to trying the food it offers. You go in and have a bite, and it's marvelous. You feel enchanted and enamored. Yet, even if the restaurant continues to provide excellent food on every visit, little by little, it will become less exciting because it becomes routine, and your brain knows what to anticipate every time. There is no novelty, no surprise, and the dopamine associated with this restaurant and its meals drop.

Dopamine always has us looking for something more and something novel rather than what we are accustomed to. The dopamine system is a brilliantly evolved mechanism that is responsible for all of mankind's questing, discovery, creation, and resilience. But can you see the problems it could cause as well? The modern world is full of temptations that affect our dopamine. Our biology simply did not evolve in the same socio-cultural environment we have created for ourselves in modern times. If you've ever experienced issues with poor motivation, addiction, bad habits, or procrastination, then you'll know just how hard life is when your dopamine balance is out of whack.

Average social media usage, across the world, is around 145 minutes per day (Statista, 2021). That means that people spend over two hours every day on popular social media websites, and the number can be even higher for many. Social media engages us in a way few other things can, and has an impact on our dopamine systems. Social media offers a never-ending stream of content, some of which can prove valuable, funny, and enjoyable. We never know when we will come upon something great, and that helps keep us engaged. Social media is also, well, social, which makes its appeal even stronger—we crave approval, connection, and affection, and social media can provide social stimuli that signal recognition or validation in the form of likes, retweets, comments, and so on.

Our dopamine systems can, essentially, be hacked by social media. We never know when to expect a notification or a fun video or something else. This ensures that we never get too accustomed, and the novelty effect remains. In essence, this is the same trick that casinos use to keep people coming back. We can find the same mechanism in things like lotteries and raffles that allow our brain to anticipate a reward to come, but not a certain one. The engineers of such sites are aware of these processes and design their interfaces specifically to target this weakness in our biochemistry. In other words, there is money to be made from exploiting the brain's reward system, thereby getting people hooked on the cheap and endless "reward" of the 24/7 news cycle and never-ending content.

But it's not just unscrupulous mega-corporations that train our brains toward addictive behavior. We can find a similar tactic in play in toxic relationships, when our partner might give us the love and affection we crave, but only sometimes, which keeps it unpredictable. Cognitive psychologists have long understood that this intermittent reward keeps us more engaged than if we had a more consistent stream of positive outcomes. Have you ever met someone who was so used to toxic relationships that they felt bored and uneasy when they found themselves in a happy, healthy one? You can bet that they had dysregulated dopamine.

Uncertain rewards delivered on a random basis can keep us hooked better than consistent reward programs, and social media designers, game designers, and other professionals know it well. Many aspects of the modern world take advantage of this "flaw" in our neural programming to keep us hooked against our best interests and disrupt the regular flow of dopamine, making us favor certain activities.

Other things can have an impact on the dopamine system in the brain. Drugs are a clear example, as many substances that become addictive hijack the dopamine pathways and make the brain release a lot more dopamine, to the point where other stimuli, like everyday pleasures, are no longer enough to make them active. People who develop substance abuse problems might find themselves unable to find pleasure elsewhere, only through increasingly high doses of their drug. But not all drugs create the same type of addiction, and we can find similar effects from things that are not regulated substances (Diana, 2011, *The Dopamine Hypothesis of Drug Addiction and Its Potential Therapeutic Value*).

Sugar and sugary foods can create a similar state. The brain gets used to operating with higher dopamine levels and also requires higher levels of sugar, so we feel weird without it. We seek sugar and, once we consume it on a regular basis, it can be hard to reduce the amount we consume. Sugar can have a similar effect on the brain as a drug, raising our dopamine levels over time and requiring higher sugar doses to feel the same comfort we used to experience (Lewis, 2017, *What Happens to Our Brain When We Give Up Sugar?*).

Extreme thrills can also raise the dopamine level. This can explain the experience of extreme athletes who feel the need to raise the stakes in their activities, because their brain gets used to operating with higher levels of dopamine, so lower-stakes activities no longer lead to the same thrill (Dominguez, 2015, *Why Are We Addicted to Extreme Ssports?*). We can find similar effects from risk-taking behaviors, some forms of sexual behaviors, and others, which makes our brain accustomed to higher levels of dopamine and make the behaviors hard to quit even if they become disruptive to our normal life or put us at some sort of risk.

Higher dopamine levels can make it harder for us to enjoy regular activities. They push us—because of the way our dopamine systems work—to strive for more and increase the intensity and the novelty associated with our day-to-day situations, which is not always feasible, productive, or even safe. Many people find themselves unable to quit social media or casual gaming, even when it stands in the way of their goals and dreams. Instant gratification—the appeal of predicting a reward soon to come—is hard to manage. It's why we fail to follow through on behaviors we know are good for us, and why we keep doing things we know are not in alignment with our values. In other words, we're dopamine junkies!

The problem we will tackle here is the issue of having too much dopamine. But what is the problem with this? Isn't dopamine good?

Its functions are more complex than just reward or anticipation. Too much dopamine can make it hard for us to focus, especially on things that do not offer quick and easy stimulation or those goals we need to work for. We become easily bored and see our attention span decreasing and withering away, so we struggle to engage with things that are longer or more challenging or take time to pay off.

High dopamine can contribute to undesirable behaviors, like acting on impulse or being more irritable and aggressive or euphoric, which can also make us make poor decisions. Excessively high dopamine levels, like the ones that come after using drugs, can even be associated with dangerous symptoms, like hallucinations, although this is not something to worry about on the regular. Too much dopamine can make it harder for us to enjoy things and to center ourselves enough to get things done (Deans, 2011, *Dopamine Primer*).

So, what can we do to hack our dopamine systems and change the ways in which we operate? Here is how we can hack our dopamine system to reduce our dopamine levels in a healthy way.

CHAPTER 1

Take Back Your Focus

Marketers of all kinds seem to have a good grasp on how to hack our dopamine systems and keep us engaged with their products. Why can't we do the same? Once we understand how the dopamine systems work, we can employ tactics to use it for good, to pursue the goals that work for us and to reduce the levels of dopamine in our brain. We can choose to keep control over our dopamine rather than hand it over to third parties, and reclaim our focus and own motivation. It's difficult to imagine a clearer example of biohacking—making the unconscious conscious and taking proactive control of your own biology.

It's important to note that we are changing our brains every day on a functional and even structural level. We are always, in a sense, hacking our biology; it's just a question of whether we're doing it consciously, whether we're doing it in our own best interests, or whether it's being done *to* us, or *by* us. Anything that we learn and any habit that we practice changes our brain thanks to neuroplasticity, a characteristic that makes each part of our brain, the way it works and the way it is structured, changeable, and our dopamine pathways are not the exception (Begega, Santin, Galeano, Cutuli, & Sampedro-Piquero, 2017, *Neuroplasticity and Healthy Lifestyle: How Can We Understand This Relationship?*).

We can change the ways in which our brain operates and take back our time and effort to focus it on things that matter by shifting our habits or choosing specific practices that can reduce the dopamine levels in the brain.

One example of an approach that can help is the so-called "dopamine detox". A detox involves intentionally trying to reduce the levels of dopamine in the brain by abstaining from specific activities. We can adopt particular habits, increase productivity, make ourselves less prone to distractions and more likely to get things done through specific techniques.

A word of caution before we move on to the techniques themselves. Dopamine is a part of our brains and an important chemical that allows us to feel motivation and seek out new things. It's not bad, nor is it something we can try to get rid of. If you do a detox, the goal is to reduce the levels of dopamine in your brain, but dopamine will always be there, and it serves an important function. It's not something to be avoided, but rather a healthy and huge part of our neural networks. We only seek to reduce its presence when it can be harmful to us and to our other goals.

Another word of caution is that the following techniques are not meant to address addictions on a clinical level. Individuals who have an addition to a specific substance should seek clinical help. There are other mechanisms involved in substance abuse problems, and a dopamine detox is unlikely to fix them. The same is true for addictions like gambling—it's best to seek professional support.

With this out of the way, let's move on to the techniques that will help you hack your dopamine systems and reclaim your motivation in a sea of endless distractions, avoiding the lure of instant gratification. You can reduce dopamine and enjoy the things you do in a more meaningful way without relying on high levels of stimulation.

It's not always easy to make a behavioral change. Dopamine is meant to attract us and be hard to give up—it is the chemical that drives us to achieve more, do better, and strive for our goals and dreams, after all. When we have high dopamine levels, it might feel harder to focus, but little by little, your brain will adjust. Here are a few general ideas that should help you gain control over your dopamine and your habits.

Make your environment help you

If you are trying to detox from your phone, your phone should not be right by you. That book you are going to read, however, ought to be kept close, where you can grab it.

Our environment is full of triggers and reminders that can push us toward specific types of behavior. If you walk by a table full of chocolate and candy, it will be more difficult to resist the temptation than if you have a table full of fruit.

Simple changes in your environment can support your changes in habits and make it much easier to avoid negative behaviors. Take a critical look around the room and consider the things that are likely to distract you, and those you might need to succeed with your goals.

Use all the tools at your disposal, and rely on other people when you can

Don't rely on just your willpower. Your willpower drains throughout the day and is likely to fail when you are under a lot of stress or tired. It can be hard to stick to your goals even if you are motivated (Baumeister et al., 2007, *The Strength Model of Self-control*). This is normal and expected, and you can reduce your reliance on willpower by changing your environment, as detailed above, and also by using helpful tools.

One of the biggest challenges is to stay away from social media, so you might use a program to block the apps or cut off the internet. You might ask another person for help and support by giving them your phone for a day. Don't be afraid to ask for help.

Get some social support and accountability

Other people can provide valuable help, but their support is also important. Tell those you trust and who are likely to support you about your goals. They will help cheer you on, understand what's going on with you, and also offer some accountability. If you tell others that you are staying off of social media for a day, you are more likely to meet this goal.

If you can find an accountability buddy or someone to share the dopamine taming process with you, that could be even better. You can relate to each other's experiences and offer emotional support for the particular challenges you are both facing. You can also make a deal with a friend who is pursuing other goals to report to each other about your progress and check in periodically. Accountability helps you stick with your goals even when things get rough (Oussedik et al., 2017, *Accountability: A Missing Construct in Models of Adherence Behavior and in Clinical Practice*).

Be compassionate to yourself

We often tend to be very harsh toward ourselves when we make a mistake. But being critical can make us more likely to give up. It is hard to give up the dopamine rushes that we experience every day and to change habits that last a long time. Being compassionate, even if we skip a day or fall back on old practices, encourages us to keep going (Biber & Ellis, 2017).

Remember that you can recover from one slip-up, but it's best to avoid a second one. Acknowledge what happened and ask yourself what you can learn from the situation. Perhaps it will help you do better next time.

Don't bite off more than you can chew

Andrew Kirby (2020, *Dopamine Detox series*) strongly suggests that you work to change your habits related to dopamine with a level you are sure you can achieve. If you feel that it would be hard to quit cold turkey, don't do it. Cut down on some activities, but not all. Success is important, as it can motivate you to keep going, because otherwise you might feel that you have proven to yourself your habits will never shift.

Set yourself up for success, not failure. Make sure you set realistic goals and take it easy; don't be afraid to adjust your goals if you find that it is necessary. Go step by step.

A few considerations and cautions

There are a few considerations associated with dopamine and the strategies we will discuss. Take everything with a critical mind and adapt to your situation. These solutions might not work well for everyone, as it's not as easy to implement a dopamine detox when you have to work every day with social media, for example, or when you have to be on your phone 24/7 because your job requires you to be prepared for emergencies. Consider what is applicable for you and what works for you—it's fine if you can't do everything detailed below.

Consider also that dopamine is not a harmful substance—it is a natural chemical in our brains that we need. When we talk about a dopamine detox or a fasting process, we are not striving to get rid of dopamine; that's impossible and not the goal at all. The goal instead is to reduce high dopamine levels associated with harmful habits, such as social media use or sugary foods, and reconnect with oneself. It involves creating a situation where you can again enjoy and prioritize your healthy habits and your own creativity rather than feel that your brain is running on its own. It is about empowering and making healthier changes, and the words "detox" and "fasting", which have become fashionable, are good metaphorical descriptions of the processes.

A dopamine fast, a detox, and other strategies outlined below are not meant to serve as solutions to a *bona fide* addiction and substance abuse problems or highly problematic behaviors like gambling. If you feel that you might be experiencing an addiction, you should seek professional help. An addiction is defined, according to the *Diagnostic and Statistical Manual of Mental Disorders* (5th edition) or DSM-5 (APA, 2013), as:

- Taking or using a substance more and for more time than you intended (engaging in a behavior like gambling for more than you intended)
- Wanting to stop but being unable to
- Spending a lot of time trying to get the substance or the means for the behavior, dealing with the consequences, thinking about it constantly
- Getting urges and cravings for the substance/behavior
- Continuing to engage in the behavior or substance even when it starts to cause problems in your relationships, work, education, or other areas
- Not being able to fulfill your responsibilities at work, in school, or at home due to the behavior or substance

- Giving up other important and valuable activities in favor of the behavior or substance
- Needing to use more or do more in order to feel the same experience

While dopamine is meant to be involved in addiction, the techniques described below are not treatments for this problem, which often requires professional support and even might need medical help. The same is true of situations when you are experiencing a disconnect with reality or other medical and psychiatric symptoms that go beyond the scope of this material.

Now, let's take a close look at all the techniques that can help us reduce our dopamine levels and gain more control over our attention, our boredom, and our motivation.

Summary

- Dopamine is a powerful and complex neurotransmitter, but the modern world can play havoc with its healthy and optimal balance. Dopamine allows us to feel pleasure and reward, experience anticipation and desire, and seek out novelty. A dysregulated dopamine system can result in significant impairment to our motivation, our ability to experience pleasure, impulse control, mood, concentration, attention, self-discipline, and desire, among other things.

- We are not at the mercy of our neurochemistry, however—the brain is plastic and can be changed if we are aware of its mechanisms and work to support it strategically.
- Part of what makes behavioral change so hard can be thought of as dopamine addiction, and consequently a "dopamine detox" can help bring more regulation to the way we process information and act in each moment.
- If dopamine is a biochemical proxy for willpower, then learning to biohack it allows us to cultivate more self-control, self-awareness, and self-regulation. We can use different techniques and methods to help improve our behavior, via the dopamine system.
- We can create an environment that is supportive of focus and attention; for example, by removing distractions like smartphones. Use apps or programs to moderate your behavior or enlist the help of others to keep you accountable to your goals.
- Lapses are inevitable, so practice compassion rather than beating yourself up. Learn from your mistakes and move on, rather than dwelling on them. Likewise, think small and don't bite off more than you can chew. Some techniques will work for you, some not. Experiment a little.

CHAPTER 2

A Detox To End Them All

A dopamine detox is a new strategy that can help you reduce the levels of dopamine your brain is used to. It's a relatively new technique that draws from existing theories and research to help you unplug and cut down on all the activities that are keeping you hooked. If you do such a detox, you'll notice that much of the vocabulary comes from the addiction world, and that's because the underlying mechanisms for "classic" addictions to things like alcohol or drugs are essentially the same as the ones keeping you hooked to online shopping, Instagram, or "doomscrolling" on your phone at night when you should be sleeping.

One of the most effective biohacks you can orchestrate for yourself is not to develop superhuman memory or bulletproof immunity, but rather to break the mental and psychological chains of dopamine tolerance. Your brain is used to receiving dopamine from "easy" activities or from activities that induce a high level of this substance. We can get the rush in a way that does not require us to work for it, and that puts us off other activities that lead to better results and are overall healthier and more purposeful, but feel too dull when compared to all the tasks that give us instant gratification. Nope, it's not an existential crisis—your dopamine system's just broken!

A dopamine detox is a tool for resetting your brain and allowing you to experience things anew. Now, even though it is called a detox, this doesn't mean that dopamine is a toxic substance or that you can purge it from your brain. It will still be there; you will just get a break from the high dopamine levels that can be difficult to manage and that keep you from doing other things (Andrew Kirby, 2020, *Dopamine Detox*). Dopamine is like insulin levels in that both need to be sensitive and operate in a finely-tuned, optimal range. The goal of dopamine hacking is to make the exquisite neuro-mechanism work *for* you. This means creating both a body and a life that are geared toward hard work, appropriate challenge, moderation, self-discipline, and the satisfaction of genuinely earned pleasure.

Here are some habits and activities that can give you dopamine, but which are not all that great for you:

- Using social media, messengers, and your phone
- Video games and mobile games
- Watching shows, movies, and consuming content in general
- Consuming pornography
- Eating high-sugar foods and snacks, junk food

- Taking stimulants—coffee, tea, chocolate, some sodas, sugary drinks, drugs
- Online shopping and browsing without purchasing
- Consuming online content that features clickbait, outrage, and other manipulative strategies

These activities tend to waste a lot of our time and create higher levels of dopamine. They're like junk food for life—they're great in the moment but lack spiritual or emotional nutrition and leave you worse off than before. It's worth noting that all rewarding activities can stimulate the release of dopamine, but the ones that offer instant gratification are especially powerful and can be hard to quit.

A dopamine detox is meant to reset your brain and allow you time to just be with yourself. It can help you explore what happens when you give up on this dopamine rush and instead allow yourself to be bored, to be alone with yourself, and let your thoughts come and go uninterrupted. Build tolerance for craving, dissatisfaction, and having to wait. It may feel like deprivation in the moment, but in fact you are building your ability to experience *more* pleasure. It's like the person who hasn't eaten junk food for years: when they taste an ultra-processed deep-fried meal, they don't enjoy it, and they genuinely find more pleasure in foods that are natural, wholesome, and less stimulating.

So, how exactly can we use these principles to make concrete changes to our lives? The first thing to get clear on is that a dopamine detox isn't, by definition, a quick fix. It's not going to feel easy, pleasant, or thrilling. But it isn't meant to be. Pay attention to any feelings you have of breezing through a one-day detox and coming out the other end magically transformed with very little effort—that's just the dopamine talking!

A 1-day detox is the best way to start the process and what Kirby describes as a "hard reset." What will you do during these 24 hours? You will not take part in any activities that stimulate your dopamine, such as the ones described above. You will not use your computer or your phone at all, you will not consume drugs or stimulants, you will not game, and you will just not engage in any activities that offer instant gratification. You're not punishing yourself. You're just removing the existential junk food from your life.

If you want to engage in this detox in an approachable way, you can cut down on these activities. The first thing you'll notice is an almost irresistible pull toward your phone, the TV, or that sugary treat. That's okay. Your head may fill with a million reasons why a detox is a stupid idea, and why you don't have to do it anymore. That's also okay. You may get depressed, angry, or bored. All normal. Just become aware of all of this and stay in the moment—you are rewiring your impulses and perceptions. Be patient. How does it feel to be so out of control, or compelled in this way? Does the world really end when you don't instantly get what you want? And really, is the thing you think you needed all that great?

In the big hole where your addictive behaviors used to be, you may suddenly feel at a loss. You can instead try spending your time:

- Meditating
- Journaling or writing
- Walking
- Reading
- Sharing with others; talking in person

If you want to make it even more challenging and get a taste of a true reset, cut out all activities except for meditating. You might even try fasting for a day. The more activities you cut out, the harder it will be, but the rewards can be greater as well. You might discover your thoughts and feelings, desires and ideas, and feel how you can be when all these distractions are not in the way.

A one-day detox is not going to resolve all ongoing issues, but it can help you give your brain a nudge and an experience that will allow you to feel ready to make bigger and more lasting changes.

You will likely feel frustrated or bored. You might reach out for your usual distractions and feel stress because you are depriving yourself of something you are accustomed to. That doesn't feel comfortable.

This is a discomfort you can tolerate. You might discover something new and unexpected about yourself and experience something that you usually don't. The discomfort will pass, and you can feel empowered by this success.

You do not have to depend on easy sources of dopamine to feel satisfied. You can shift toward more productive things, like reflection, creation rather than consumption, and others, setting goals that will motivate you in a deeper and more meaningful way.

Writing a book is deeply satisfying. It's not easy and it takes time, but it offers a more lasting source of pride, meaning, and joy than a YouTube video or a TikTok binge.

Working out regularly is not just satisfying; it can also make a huge positive difference for your health. But exercise is often not a source of instant gratification, because it can be painful and hard and require effort. The effects will be felt over time, and the long-term gratification is likely to be great if we can hold on for long enough.

Consider what habits and goals you could pursue that are not working as well due to your focus on instant gratification. What could you accomplish if you were truly focused, energized, and had enough time?

A one-day detox is a first step toward new and better habits. But a one-time detox is unlikely to work without further follow-up.

A three-day detox can be a more challenging task and can help you recognize the habits you want to keep. It would involve a similar approach to a one-day detox, eliminating all the thrills and stimulants that keep your dopamine levels up, especially things like social media, drugs including caffeine, and more; however, a three-day detox might require you to be less stringent and, in particular, not do things like fasting. However, after one day, you can consider and reflect the habits you want to bring back to your life in a more mindful way.

Three days can allow you the chance to see how you feel without your social media or coffee for longer and whether these things are worth reintroducing into your life.

Ask yourself whether these things bring value and whether you truly miss them or just miss the satisfaction and gratification they brought. How do you feel in their absence? How focused are you? What happens when you bring them back, and how does your focus shift?

A 7-day detox plan

For a 7-day detox plan, you will pick one day per week to do a detox. It's usually better to do it during the weekend, as work might depend on your ability to answer your emails or use your phone and computer. Choose a day every week to perform a reset and disconnect from all the activities that demand your attention. It will help you stay mindful and aware of the instant gratification activities and focus on your goals and ideas. As you do it more, you might discover the type of tasks and activities that best fit your situation and your needs.

Some people take a detox to its logical extreme: they fast, or they cut contact with others. You don't need to do that unless you feel it would be beneficial. Simply cutting out the most thrilling and extreme experiences for a while should be enough to feel the effects of a detox.

The most extreme version that might bring to mind a hermit or an ascetic, however, is also there if you would like the challenge. It confronts you with your own ideas and beliefs in a strong way and might leave you unsettled or uncomfortable.

Remember that it's not a good idea to push yourself too far beyond your limits, so you can try building up to this experience by trying something else first. Try the milder version and see how you feel. Cut out more activities for a day. Eventually, you might be ready for a day spent doing nothing but meditating, thinking, and being with yourself.

Dopamine fasting

Dopamine fasting is a term that is often used interchangeably with the concept of a dopamine detox. We can define dopamine fasting as the process of long-term change in dopamine-related habits, while a detox is a short-term practice. Fasting is another way to bring down the levels of dopamine in your brain and to increase your focus.

Dopamine fasting is becoming popular and allows you to regularly cut down on dopamine-heavy activities to regain your own time and focus. As it is meant to be, it is less intense than a dopamine detox, which can lead you to cut down a wide variety of behaviors, and is usually focused more on specific problematic behaviors, as outlined by Dr. Cameron Seraph (2019, *The Definitive Guide to Dopamine Fasting 2.0 — The Hot Silicon Valley Trend*).

Dopamine fasting is focused on reducing specific problematic behaviors and increasing the activities that are good, value-aligned, and healthy for you, like exercising, socializing, and so on.

The suggested times for shifting impulsive behaviors through dopamine fasting involve doing at least one or more hours of fasting every day, plus one weekend day, one weekend every quarter, and one week every year. The suggestion is to shift one's environment for the longer fasts, going on a trip, or spending the day outside and away from the temptations of the modern home. If you are doing the process and you still live with your family who are not engaged in any kind of issue, going outside might be even better, as other people's activities can take you away from your time of relaxation and unplugging. The outside makes these temptations easier to manage and also provides you enough stimulation to keep you active rather than bored out of your skull (not that boredom is necessarily a bad thing).

Sometimes, you can't give up a specific behavior. For example, maybe your family watches a show together or you still need access to your smartphone. The idea is to cut down on the time and space you give this behavior. Limit it and lay down clear boundaries:

- You can only check social media for fifteen minutes every day
- You use your smartphone in the evening right before dinner
- You watch one episode of the show with your partner

Place clear limits with regards to time and enforce them; don't be afraid to tell others what you are doing and how you are doing it. Use timers to check it and apps that monitor your behavior, too, if you tend to get engrossed. It's a good idea to have clear triggers for each behavior that mark the beginning and also the end. For example:

- You take out your phone after dinner
- You send messages while you wait for your ride
- You watch a show between 7:00 and 7:30 and stop after a single episode

You can target any problematic behaviors that keep you hooked and are causing your distress. Through fasting, you reduce your dependence on these behaviors. When you engage in fasting, having clear limits will also help others take you seriously and offer more support for your decision.

Unlike a dopamine detox, Dr. Seraph does not suggest that you give up all activities during the fast. However, he suggests that it's important to focus on regular and pleasant activities that reflect your goals and values, such as exercising, creating, making, cleaning, and so on. Dedicate the space for activities that align with your goals, like learning a new and desirable skill or working on your art.

Dopamine fasting is meant to be sustainable, so it's important that you choose a strategy that works for you and a timeline that is realistic. Don't try to simply cut out all dopamine sources and instead focus on problematic behaviors that are hurting you in some way. This will help you reduce dopamine levels more effectively without necessarily losing the enjoyment other, healthy activities bring you, too.

Mindfulness and awareness

Mindfulness is a practice that can help you reduce mindless engagement with different activities and cut down on the search for instant gratification. It can be especially useful for activities that waste time and tend to capture your attention, such as gaming or scrolling through social media. Mindfulness helps you reduce impulsive behavior and trains your brain to avoid impulsive shifts in attention like the ones associated with a high level of dopamine. As such, it can serve as a way to relax and lower the levels of dopamine by delaying instant gratification and reducing the impatience and stress that can make these jump.

Marketers and designers of all kinds often make products and services that are easy to use and easy to get addicted to, at least to some degree. There are many different aspects of social media, for instance, that make it addictive, like infinite scrolling or red notifications that make you want to check them now. Even other services, like Netflix, have some functions that make it easy to just keep going—a streaming service will start playing one episode after the next one to promote binge watching.

Mindfulness can serve as a solution—an antidote for mindless consumption and routines that lead to easy dopamine releases and instant gratification. In particular, mindful consumption can help the individual focus on the things that matter to them and that help satisfy their needs in a positive way. Mindless consumption is driven by the desire to satisfy specific needs, like the learned need for rewards and instant gratification. Mindfulness can counteract with and refocus the individual's consumption habits on things that are valuable and positive for them (Armour, 2019, *From Mindless to Consumer to Mindful Citizen: Reimagining Consumer, Societal and Environmental Sustainability*).

Mindfulness involves being present without judgment and paying attention to one's internal sensations and the external stimuli. It means focusing one's full attention on what is happening now, what you are feeling, and what the experience is. Mindfulness can help with disrupting routines of mindlessly following your habits, especially with things like social media, TV viewing, and so on. Ask yourself whether the experience is offering you something valuable. Are you enjoying yourself? What do you feel? What are your sensations? (Milne, Villarroel Ordenes, & Kaplan, 2020, *Mindful Consumption: Three Consumer Segment Views*).

The goal of mindful consumption is not to stop using all social media or consuming nothing else, instead choosing to meditate all the time. Instead, it is meant to help you experience and consume things that have value for you and that bring you genuine enjoyment or learning (Milne, Villarroel Ordenes, & Kaplan, 2020, *Mindful Consumption: Three Consumer Segment Views*).

Cultivating mindfulness can be done simply by paying attention to one's experiences in the moment. When you remember to do it or when you choose to do it, you can practice mindfulness by trying to pay full attention to what you are experiencing.

Another way is to practice mindfulness meditation—a more structured way of doing it. Developing this skill can lead to marked improvements and reduce the craving for meaningless content and instant gratification. Consuming mindfully also empowers you to stop what you are doing and make the choice of whether you want to continue, rather than following your momentary impulse. Mindfulness is also proven to increase enjoyment and improve satisfaction with different life experiences, which can help you shift habits towards more meaningful long-term gratification. Mindfulness is a good supporting strategy for reducing dopamine levels and serves as a useful foundation for other techniques, like using boredom.

Using boredom

Boredom is an undesirable state, generally speaking. We don't like being bored and will do many things to keep it away. Podcasts, music, our phones, emotional eating, and more are all options that help us fight boredom through dopamine. You can use this state, however, to your advantage. Boredom reduces dopamine because there is no stimulation, but at the same time can encourage us to try new things and helps our brain get active, rather than just consume easy content as it is presented.

Boredom can spark productivity and creativity and can also help you enjoy more tasks that involve a lower level of stimulation. We can perform better in terms of creativity after we face some degree of boredom and can enjoy things more deeply.

Boredom can be defined as a search for neural stimulation—we want something that will engage our brain. When this is not found, our brain can create stimulation through our imagination, problem-solving, and creative ability.

Often, we don't allow ourselves to feel bored, not even for a minute, and that creates a certain degree of stress and can strain our mental health. Boredom can provide an opportunity to recharge and help engage more mindfully (Ducharme, 2019, *Being Bored Can Be Good for You—If You Do It Right. Here's How*).

How can you use boredom in your favor? Allow yourself to be without stimulation. Let your mind wander and go to different places, see what ideas and thoughts pop into your head when you are not really trying too hard to engage with anything (Ducharme, 2019, *Being Bored Can Be Good for You—If You Do It Right. Here's How*).

It's easier to let your mind wander when you are doing something familiar, easy, and not stimulating, like walking or sitting. Do not have any stimulation, like music or social media or anything else (Ducharme, 2019, *Being Bored Can Be Good for You—If You Do It Right. Here's How*).

It can be difficult and stressful at first, especially as we are not accustomed to boredom. Indeed, phones and other devices reduce our tolerance for boredom and, ironically, reduce our own creativity and ability to cope with being on our own.

You can practice boredom in many situations. Let yourself not be connected, and try not to scroll or text or chat the next time you are waiting in line or on your commute. Challenge yourself to be bored for 5, 10, 15, or more minutes and see how activities feel after this period of boredom.

Try being bored for a bit before starting an activity where you need to be creative or when you will focus on an activity that involves a lower stimulation level. See how your perception of this activity changes.

Don't be afraid of boredom—it is something that stimulates your brain and allows you to jumpstart your imagination. It can also change the way in which your brain responds to activities that don't provide instant gratification. It can help you reduce dopamine by withholding the stimulation that makes our brain feel all hyped up and entertained.

Focusing on the process

Another important consideration is the matter of results and rewards. Rewards can maintain a high level of dopamine. We want that funny image, that shiny car, that A+ grade, and so much more. It's easy enough to anticipate a dopamine hit from a cute video and receive it right away. The entire process can take less than a minute and habituates us to instant gratification: I see it—I want it—I get it—I move on.

This is a process that is fine and good for a lot of things, but that can hold us back in others. For example, building an exercise habit takes time and involves a lot of unpleasantness in the beginning. Once you go out for a run for the first few times, you are likely to come back home feeling pain and exhaustion, rather than something pleasant. You are also unlikely to see any changes—running and doing exercise impacts you positively over the course of several weeks. You might notice small changes in your mood, energy, and so on, but if you exercise to lose weight, for example, you won't see shifts for a while.

The habit of exercising can become rewarding after some time. So can long-term projects involving arts, personal and professional development, learning, building skills and more that take a long time to provide dopamine, because we take a long time to see results.

If we are looking for results in all the things we do, we might struggle to create and build habits that don't produce results for a long time. For instance, if you want to write a book, you have to learn to write, edit, and so on. If you are focused only on the end result—the book—as a source of dopamine and motivation, you will be waiting a while. It might leave you feeling like you are too far from your goals for them to matter, and this is true of many of the best things we want to do. They take time, discipline, and effort.

When we focus on results, we might put ourselves at a disadvantage, because we wait for the situation to end and for the results to make themselves apparent. This limits the amount of dopamine that we can receive from many habits and can reduce our desire to do the things we need to do to make progress.

Instead of focusing on the results, we can focus on the process to increase motivation, productivity, and reduce our dopamine levels when these become too much in anticipation of the reward and begin killing our focus.

How can focusing on the process support our ultimate goal of bringing down dopamine levels? It allows us to lower dopamine levels in anticipation of a reward and instead focus on what we are doing and deriving enjoyment from the activity. It can push us to pay attention and, while we are focused on the process, to avoid distractions that can add to the irritability and overall distractibility. It brings dopamine down and helps us get used to working without the promise of an immediate or upcoming reward that comes with a dopamine high.

When you focus more on the process, you can achieve several benefits that increase the satisfaction you face and even the outcomes.

A focus on results often suggests the possibility of failure. If you don't do as well as you want, you might be disappointed. Disappointment is a state produced by a failure to predict an adequate reward and, as such, leads to a negative state (in contrast with a pleasant surprise that increases the amount of dopamine our brain releases). Some people only need a small experience with disappointment to be unwilling to take risks or pursue results (Tzieropolous et al., 2011, *The Impact of Disappointment in Decision Making: Inter-individual*

Differences and Electrical Neuroimaging). While this might appear as a good thing when seeking to reduce dopamine levels, in practice, it drives us to the other extreme and can put a big dent in our plans for self-improvement and growth.

When you focus on the process, you can save yourself the disappointment. You will fulfill the goal anyway and reduce the likelihood of being demotivated by the results not being up to snuff.

Another benefit is that it allows you to immerse yourself and feel in the flow state, a state that is linked to more balanced dopamine levels, increased creativity and satisfaction, and a higher life quality. Flow states are linked to positive effects on the mind and the body (Gold & Ciorciari, 2020, *A Review on the Role of the Neuroscience of Flow States in the Modern World*).

A flow state occurs when you allow yourself to pay full attention to what you are doing, not really caring about the outcomes. A flow state is characterized by (Gold & Ciorciari, 2020, *A Review on the Role of the Neuroscience of Flow States in the Modern World*):

- Optimal and smooth performance
- Full attention directed at the activity
- Reduced awareness of other thoughts and yourself, including negative thoughts, ideas, or doubts
- Feeling like time is flying by, losing the awareness of time passing (hours go by quickly)

When you enter a flow state, you are operating at your best level. Something important is that it allows you to be creative and productive without worrying about doing well or doing badly.

How can you achieve a flow state? By focusing on the process. Here is what this entails:

First, you need to give yourself time. You need to take some time without distractions to truly experience it. In order to manage this, there are two basic techniques that can help you.

The Pomodoro technique

The Pomodoro technique is a technique that involves focusing on the process by dividing your work into chunks of time: traditionally, 25-minute chunks with 5-minute breaks. You can set a timer to remind you of the Pomodoros and immerse yourself in the task. If you get nothing done, it's fine; take your break and try again. The goal, however, is to focus on whatever you are doing and reduce distractions during the 25 minutes. Dedicate your full attention for this time to whatever it is you want to do (Cirillo, 2006, *The Pomodoro Technique*).

The Pomodoro technique does not work for every situation or every type of work. Some people find that they need to constantly shift their attention or feel that the Pomodoro does not support focus as much as it should. You can experiment; for instance, try shorter or longer periods of uninterrupted work, see whether playing relaxing instrumental music helps you focus, and more.

Some people prefer to do time blocking or timeboxing instead of Pomodoro. They use the same approach for planning your whole day and even your whole workweek.

Time blocking

Time blocking is similar to the Pomodoro technique, but goes beyond to promote flow states and a deeper focus on the process. It encourages you to divide your day into blocks of time (also called timeboxes) and schedule for each of these blocks only one type of activity (Scroggs, 2021, *Time Blocking*).

For example:

10:00 a.m. — 2:00 p.m.	Develop new client proposal
12:00 p.m. — 1:00 p.m.	Lunch break
1:00 p.m. — 2:00 p.m.	Check and answer emails and messages
2:00 p.m. — 5:00 p.m.	Work on new project

Time blocking allows you to truly get in the zone and work doing your best efforts, immersed in the activity. It becomes more enjoyable, challenging, and reduces the amount of stress and resources it takes to shift between activities (Scroggs, 2021, *Time Blocking*).

Time blocking is a relatively recent proposal that has shown to lead to better outcomes at work and in other situations, and it is also a useful strategy for focusing on the process and allowing results to improve on their own, without worrying or stressing about quality (Scroggs, 2021, *Time Blocking*).

A flow state can help us forget about rewards and distractions to reduce dopamine levels overall.

Create a challenge

Some tasks can be pretty boring on their own. If they take a long time, you might find your mind drifting away and focusing on other things instead, which can take you away from the process. A way of improving your flow state here is to create a challenge for yourself.

Challenge yourself to do things faster or better or in a different way from what you are used to. Even boring tasks can become a bit more engaging and create a challenge that promotes a state of flow when you are setting your own goals in addition to the ones associated with the task.

Imagine that you need to organize your desk. Challenge yourself to do it in under 30 minutes, get rid of half of all the papers you have waiting there, or to redo the whole thing. Even if you are not thrilled by the idea of cleaning, you can enjoy it a lot more and stay more focused when there is an additional level of difficulty.

You can also try making the task into a game. Even boring and monotonous tasks can be engaging when they are approached as a game with points or a fun framing within your mind. Imagine yourself as a secret agent who needs to avoid arousing suspicion, or as an alien who needs to blend in by having just the perfect human desk. Using your imagination and creativity can make any process more rewarding and create a flow state where there was previously only boredom or frustration.

A flow state is associated with higher levels of dopamine and is rewarding to us on its own. An important consideration to achieve this flow state is the need to reduce distractions.

Make sure to shut off any notifications and avoid messaging, checking your email, and other distracting activities as much as you can. Try to immerse yourself in the process and enjoy it.

Shifting your focus to the process rather than the results can keep you motivated and improve your performance. It means that you do not depend on getting a specific outcome to feel rewarded by what you have accomplished.

Celebrating your achievements

Even though in your day to day you want to focus on the process, at some point, you do want to consider the results as well as the process. Specifically, you can celebrate the results you achieve once you recognize some progress. But there are some obstacles in relation to this, too.

Often, we fail to recognize our achievements and do not receive the associated dopamine. Even when our main goal is to reduce its levels, we cannot do without dopamine, and it's better to receive it from sources that will encourage us to do better and to be better, and to keep going with our healthier habits and achievements. We might have something to provide us with a reward, but we need to pay attention and recognize it as such.

When you celebrate your achievement, you halt the cycle of wanting more for a brief period of time. The anticipation pays off, and you can simply be in the moment. It brings down the levels of dopamine associated with the constant striving for more and teaches you to find satisfaction in the present. Over time, it can bring down the dopamine levels that make you rush to find the next best thing and instead focus on what is happening.

One common obstacle for this is perfectionism: no matter how well you did, you could have done better. Perfectionism can make us afraid to look at our own work with pride and recognize, much less celebrate everything that we have achieved.

Perfectionism can make us less motivated and devalue our achievements because we feel that they are not good enough or do not pass the internal bar that we have set. This means that even when we do well, we do not recognize our achievements but instead focus on the negative aspects, which leads to disappointment and, due to this, a dip in dopamine and a loss of motivation (Tzieropolous et al., 2011, *The Impact of Disappointment in Decision Making: Inter-individual Differences and Electrical Neuroimaging*).

Counteracting perfectionism, however, is easier than it seems. It involves making a conscious effort to celebrate, recognize, and enjoy our achievements without devaluing them. We can use the idea of a feedback loop to create a virtuous circle that motivates us to keep going.

When we reach a result, we can focus on the feelings of success it brings, even if it is a small or intermediate step. But from these feelings of success, we can keep going forward to reach more and better goals each time (Lukens, 2015, *How to Tap into the Neuroscience of Winning*).

Even if your accomplishment was small, take a moment to become aware. Allow yourself to experience the feel-good sensation of doing, of achieving. Often, we stop ourselves short by bringing ourselves down (e.g., "It wasn't a big deal," or "Anyone could have done it," or "It could have been done much better") or not allowing our brain to enjoy the situation. We can sometimes worry that indulging will make us complacent, but that's not true—it can give us more motivation to try and achieve new things in the future (Lukens, 2015, *How to Tap into the Neuroscience of Winning*).

When you celebrate an achievement, your brain also focuses on everything that you did to reach this point and provides you a stronger incentive to repeat these same actions in the future (Guthridge, 2019, *Recently Succeed at Something? Celebrating Is Good for Your Brain*).

It starts with awareness: what are you celebrating? How can you acknowledge it? You can find a way to mark this achievement; for instance, by marking it in a calendar in a special way, writing about it, sharing it with friends and loved ones, or getting a small token for the celebration, like a fancy drink or a dessert. Celebrating with others can make the experience feel more real, especially if others join you in your excitement (Guthridge, 2019, *Recently Succeed at Something? Celebrating Is Good for Your Brain*).

You can find a group of like-minded individuals and create regular opportunities to celebrate each other. For example, if you meet once a week or once every two weeks, the end of the meeting can be dedicated to everyone sharing their achievements and being applauded without criticism or doubt. Social validation can add a lot to the dopamine rush we experience from our achievements and can make it all feel a lot more solid (Guthridge, 2019, *Recently Succeed at Something? Celebrating Is Good for Your Brain*).

If something like that is not an option, celebrate with yourself. Get a special treat to mark the occasion, do a victory dance, take a well-earned break—experiment to find whatever method that works for you and leaves you feeling satisfied and happy with everything you have accomplished (Guthridge, 2019, *Recently Succeed at Something? Celebrating Is Good for Your Brain*).

Celebration is an antidote to perfectionism and the tendency to devalue one's achievements. Another option for maximizing positive emotions is the practice of gratitude.

Gratitude involves recognizing and appreciating what you have, what you enjoyed, and what you have achieved. By keeping a regular record of everything that we have to be thankful for, we train our brains to focus more on the positives and recognize them. Gratitude can amplify positive emotions, including those related to achievement, which can bring about a positive cycle of reinforcement and motivation rather than feeling disappointed or giving up (Magno & Orillosa, 2012, *Gratitude and Achievement Emotions*).

Gratitude and celebration are focused on helping you become aware of everything that you are accomplishing and recognize your progress. There is another important antidote, though, to perfectionism that we can consider and employ. This is the practice of self-compassion. Let's examine it in more detail.

Self-compassion is a healthy way of relating to oneself that can be cultivated and that can reduce the impact of perfectionism. In particular, it can shield us from disappointment in ourselves and even serve as a protective factor against depression. Self-compassion means being open to understanding one's own suffering and allowing one to feel kindness and caring toward oneself. It means taking a non-judgmental approach even as we recognize our flaws or mistakes and work to do better. Self-compassion involves recognizing our own experience as a part of the larger human experience, mindfully, without singling ourselves as uniquely bad or incapable (Ferrari, Yap, Scott, Einstein, & Ciarrochi, 2018, *Self-compassion Moderates the Perfectionism and Depression Link in Both Adolescence and Adulthood*).

Self-compassion consists of three basic elements. First, there is self-kindness, which opposes self-criticism and allows us to avoid negative labels and judgments. Then, there is common humanity, which involves connecting to other people rather than isolating oneself or feeling bad. The third element is mindfulness, which involves focusing on the experience as it is without judgment (Ferrari, Yap, Scott, Einstein, & Ciarrochi, 2018, *Self-compassion Moderates the Perfectionism and Depression Link in Both Adolescence and Adulthood*). We have discussed mindfulness, so we will focus on self-compassion and its other components.

Self-compassion means being open to one's pain and painful experiences and treating yourself without harshness or criticism. It allows the person to extend kindness to themselves even when they recognize that something is lacking. It allows you to accept yourself as you are as you move toward improvements (Ferrari, Yap, Scott, Einstein, & Ciarrochi, 2018, *Self-compassion Moderates the Perfectionism and Depression Link in Both Adolescence and Adulthood*).

How can you cultivate self-compassion? You can focus on reducing your critical self-talk. Acknowledge how you talk to yourself when you make a mistake or do something that you regret. Acknowledge that you are being critical and try to reduce the harshness of the words you are using. Imagine you were talking to a dear friend—how would you talk to them if they made a mistake? This usually helps you feel kinder and less harsh (Neff, 2021, *Self-Compassion Guided Practices and Exercises*).

Recognize your suffering and pain and allow it to come. Do not judge yourself for what you are experiencing and offer yourself some kindness. What would you like to hear? What could reassure you?

Provide yourself with the words and actions you would like to see from other people (Neff, 2021, *Self-Compassion Guided Practices and Exercises*).

People often fear practicing self-compassion, as they expect it will make them sloppier in their work or make them unwilling to change. But the best and most lasting change comes from a place of self-acceptance and self-love.

Self-compassion can help you shift your habits and also support your work toward reducing the engagement you have with high-dopamine activities and support you if at any point you experience a fallback. Like mindfulness, it is another base strategy that can help you get through the difficult stages of working to reduce dopamine levels and the frustration or boredom or falling off the wagon it can sometimes entail.

Actionable lifestyle shifts

We have been talking about behavioral shifts that can help you with dopamine. Some address dopamine directly, like dopamine detoxing and fasting, which allow you to take a break from high dopamine levels. Some address dopamine in indirect ways, too. In addition to our behaviors and habits, however, our dopamine levels can be influenced by lifestyle factors, which also impact how sensitive our brain becomes to dopamine, how it releases dopamine, and how easy or difficult it is for us to change our habits or to fall into the instant gratification trap. Let's examine the influence of biological and physiological factors on dopamine and how our daily habits of sleeping, eating, exercising, and more can influence dopamine. Here are some healthy habits, lifestyle shifts, and practical techniques you can use to bring dopamine down and keep it at a lower baseline level.

Sleep

Dopamine has many functions and is, among other things, involved in the regulation of the sleep and wakefulness cycle. In particular, it is related to the regulation of wakefulness and can be influenced by a lack of adequate sleep.

A single night without sleep can increase the amount of dopamine in the brain. Dopamine promotes wakefulness, and it can be difficult to fall asleep due to higher levels. At the same time, it suggests that not sleeping well can lead to problems with dopamine and increased levels of the substance, which also has implications for cognitive performance and the reaction to different habits (Society for Neuroscience, 2008, *One Sleepless Night Increases Dopamine in the Human Brain*).

If we are trying to reduce dopamine levels and, in particular, perform a fast or a detox, it is important to ensure we are sleeping well, as not sleeping enough can lead to higher levels of dopamine in the brain and difficulties sleeping, which can lead to a vicious cycle.

In addition to this, sleep is important for our self-control. Good sleep habits allow us to replenish and maintain self-control, while sleep deprivation can lead to impulsivity, difficulties paying attention, difficulties tolerating frustration and boredom, and compromised decision making (Pilcher, Morris, Donnelly, & Feigl, *Interactions Between Sleep Habits and Self-control*). This means that a lack of sleep can make it a lot harder for us to engage in the dopamine-changing habits we want to promote because these often require higher self-control. It's easier to choose to watch a cat video than to meditate, so sleep deprivation means that our urge for instant gratification can win over our long-term goals.

Sleep deprivation has a lot of other negative effects on our health that can complicate our pursuits of a healthier and better life.

Sleeping well means getting an average of 8 or so hours of sleep per night, maintaining a regular sleep schedule, and having a high sleep quality, measured by feeling rested and focused in the mornings.

Nutrition

Nutrition can help us increase our dopamine levels in a healthy way without relying on excessive lows and highs, such as the ones caused by sugary foods and stimulants. While each person's diet is highly dependent on their personal situation and physiology, here are some concrete tips that can help you create a diet plan that supports your goals.

Now, sugary foods and drinks that have caffeine often help us experience a dopamine high. The high lasts a short time, however, and makes our brain used to the stimulant (requiring higher doses of sugar and caffeine, which can have negative effects on our bodies and health), and the effects drop quickly, leaving us tired instead. It's better to include more products that provide sustainable support for dopamine production and are good for us.

Dopamine can be improved by foods that are rich in tyrosine, an amino acid found in almonds, fish, and chicken. Fermented foods that contain probiotics, such as kefir, also appear to be beneficial for dopamine (Ohwovoriole, 2021, *7 Natural Ways to Increase Your Dopamine Levels*). A diet incorporating foods high in protein and in tyrosine, like turkey, eggs, dairy, soy, and legumes, can impact our brain a positive way and reduce how much dopamine we need to produce because it becomes more freely available, while having not enough protein can make it more of a problem (Julson, 2018, *10 Best Ways to Increase Dopamine Levels Naturally*).

The foods that are high in tyrosine often also have a high protein content, which makes them a good addition to many diets. In addition, they have a link to better cognitive performance, for a bonus. Here are some foods that have high tyrosine content (Kuhn et al., 2017, *Food for Thought: Association Between Dietary Tyrosine and Cognitive Performance in Younger and Older Adults*):

- Cheese and dairy products
- Soy and soybeans
- Beef, lamb, pork
- Fish (especially salmon)
- Chicken
- Nuts
- Eggs
- Whole grains

In addition to these, products like avocados can help us overcome disappointments because they contain dopamine, as do bananas, plantains, and banana peels (Briguglio et al., 2018, *Dietary Neurotransmitters: A Narrative Review on Current Knowledge*). These might be foods to avoid when feeling particularly high on dopamine. On the other hand, foods like oranges, tomatoes, aubergines, spinach, and peas have low dopamine content when compared with other plants (Briguglio et al., 2018, *Dietary Neurotransmitters: A Narrative Review on Current Knowledge*).

If you are looking for supplements that might help you overcome strong dips in dopamine and keep it stable, while working to reduce the overall levels of dopamine, there is some evidence that supplements like magnesium and omega-3 can help with dopamine production. It might not be a good idea to take them when irritated or distracted, but they can help your brain have more dopamine available in situations of boredom or stress (Shen et al., 2019, *Treatment of Magnesium-L-Threonate Elevates the Magnesium Level in The Cerebrospinal Fluid and Attenuates Motor Deficits and Dopamine Neuron Loss in a Mouse Model of Parkinson's Disease*; Sublette et al., 2014, *Polyunsaturated Fatty acid Associations with Dopaminergic Indices in Major Depressive Disorder*).

Generally speaking, a healthy diet is more likely to promote more stable dopamine levels. It is not likely to be the determining factor, though. In particular, try to increase the levels of protein in your diet and reduce the consumption of things like alcohol, coffee, sugar, and stimulants that can cause your dopamine levels to rise and drop.

Exercise

Exercising is another natural way to raise your dopamine and stabilize it. Physical exercise can improve the release of dopamine and promote a better situation (APA, 2020, *https://www.apa.org/topics/exercise-fitness/stress*).

When we talk about exercise, we don't mean a particular type of activity or even a specific level of physical activity. Increasing your physical activity should have a positive effect on your mental and physical health, and also allow you to get less dopamine, but receive it from activities that are good for you rather than those that induce distraction. Exercise can improve your focus, boost your energy levels, and allow a host of other benefits that can also make you feel like you are doing something good and useful—because you are.

Try walking or dancing or jogging or any type of physical activity that brings you more pleasure than stress. Don't get overwhelmed, as even 5 or 15 minutes of exercise can make a difference. Seek tasks that are enjoyable and easy to do, especially when you first integrate exercise into your daily routine. So, if you hate jogging, try something else first.

It's also useful to try and make exercise a social activity. Find groups or friends who can do it with you—this will not only increase accountability but can also boost the pleasure you get from exercising in general.

Relaxation techniques

Relaxation can be an asset in our journey to train our brain to live with less dopamine overall. Relaxation techniques offer solutions for those situations when we feel bored and frustrated and help us avoid the impulsive choice. In addition to this, stress can boost dopamine levels, but not in a good way. It makes it overall less sensitive to good things and also makes us irritable and anxious rather than motivated or pleased (Baik, 2020, *Stress and the Dopaminergic Reward System*). Relaxation techniques are an easy solution to stress that you can implement when needed. Some are more complex than others, but generally, all of these take only a few minutes to put into practice.

The goal of these techniques is to bring down your stress levels and associated levels of dopamine. Stress can stimulate the release of dopamine, too, and make us less sensitive to the small things in life, rather than needing quick and easy fixes to get our doses. Relaxation can counteract stress and bring down the dopamine levels linked to this problem, ensuring that we are less irritable, distracted, and unfocused.

Progressive muscle relaxation

Progressive muscle relaxation involves a simple technique when you tense a group of muscles as you breathe in. You keep them tense for 4 to 10 seconds and then breathe out and relax the muscle group. Then you take a few seconds to relax and tense another muscle group as you breathe in and relax them as you breathe out. Notice how your muscles feel when they tense and how they feel when they relax (Toussaint et al., 2021, *Effectiveness of Progressive Muscle Relaxation, Deep Breathing, and Guided Imagery in Promoting Psychological and Physiological States of Relaxation*).

What is a muscle group? It is a cluster of muscles; therefore, working through each group progressively means clenching a single part of your body and then moving on to the next one. Muscle relaxation can include going from your toes up to the top of your head, or the other way around (University of Michigan, 2020, *Stress Management: Doing Progressive Muscle Relaxation*).

Box breathing

Box breathing or square breathing is a quick and easy antidote to stress. It consists of breathing in and out, slowly. You inhale on the count of four, hold your breath on a count of four, exhale on a count of four, and hold your breath before inhaling once more, all counting to four (Toussaint et al., 2021, *Effectiveness of Progressive Muscle Relaxation, Deep Breathing, and Guided Imagery in Promoting Psychological and Physiological States of Relaxation*; Gotter, 2020, *Box Breathing*).

Box breathing is easy to practice anywhere, and it really works.

Visualization and guided imagery

Visualization and guided imagery refer to a series of techniques when you imagine pleasant visual images that relax you. When you do visualization, you do it on your own, while in guided imagery, you use an audio or video guide, or someone else walks you through it (Toussaint et al., 2021, *Effectiveness of Progressive Muscle Relaxation, Deep Breathing, and Guided Imagery in Promoting Psychological and Physiological States of Relaxation*).

Find a relaxing scene that evokes pleasant emotions and experiences. For some, it's a beach; for others, a childhood home. Make sure the voice, if you are doing guided imagery, is comfortable for you. Try to imagine it in a lot of detail, bringing in all your senses: what are the smells and the sensations on your skin; what can you hear? Imagining scenes with blue and green, like the sky or a meadow, help more than colors like red or orange.

You can build your own scene and bring yourself back to a comfortable space when you need it. Take your time to build an imaginary space that is detailed—one you can go back to time and again when things get rough.

Autogenic training

Autogenic training is another simple technique. You just need to sit in a comfortable position in a place where you can speak to yourself. Take a few minutes to breathe deeply, using your belly or abdomen rather than your chest. Say to yourself that you are calm.

Focus your attention on your arms and repeat to yourself, out loud, but slowly and quietly: "My arms are very heavy." Repeat it six times and say to yourself that you are calm. Then repeat six times that your arms are warm. Do the same for your legs and for your abdomen. Focus on your breathing and repeat to yourself that your breathing is slow and that you are calm (Cuncic, 2020, *Autogenic Training for Reducing Anxiety*; Stetter & Kupper, 2002, *Autogenic Training: a Meta-analysis of Clinical Outcome Studies*).

You can use other commands with autogenic training. The goal is to pair deep breathing and spoken instructions to help you feel relaxed. You can choose to use other phrases that help you feel relaxed, just make sure to breathe deeply as you do.

Relaxation techniques will help you regulate your stress and reduce dopamine in your body.

Choice management

We have talked about changes you can make to your own habits, but let's revisit for a bit the way in which you can reduce the attractiveness of instant gratification choices, like using social media, apps, or games. You can take some measures to make the easy choices you want to reduce less appealing for you and less likely to distract you. Make these choices simpler and better and work to reduce your dopamine levels for the long haul to make it more effortless.

What is the role of choice management in bringing down dopamine levels? It helps make the stimuli most strongly tied to increased dopamine levels less available and, as a result, more possible to resist. It helps us withstand that space when we might still crave our old distractions and wean our brain off of excessively high dopamine levels.

Make it inaccessible

The first strategy is to limit your access to social media, apps, the internet, or specific sites that are likely to be time-wasters. You probably know what they are. Move your computer or devices out of the bedroom for the evening or night, for instance, or keep them far away from your bed if you are likely to reach for them once your willpower levels deplete.

Another solution is to install apps that can block you from using specific sites or social media for specific periods of time and customize it according to your needs. Some apps are strict enough that they will not allow any access or make it difficult to do so. Even having to log out and log in every time you want to use something can create a space where you get to ask yourself whether you truly want to do it.

The same goes for things like food or stimulants or other temptations. Make sure you put them away or don't buy them when you want to cut down on these habits. Put them in some difficult-to-reach place—this means they are still there, but you will have to be really mindful of your choice to consume them and also have to make more of an effort to reach them, which can make it less appealing as an easy dose of dopamine. If you feel this wouldn't work, consider whether you have ever had vegetables or fruit spoiling in the bottom drawer of your fridge, or forgotten snacks languishing in the back of your pantry. The harder something is to reach, the less likely we are to use it.

Take control of when you do something

Schedule everything in advance. If you know you will get a half an hour with your social media apps in the evening, it can help you reduce temptation and makes it easier to resist the pull to try and use them before. If you plan for a fancy dessert on the weekend, you can weather a difficult Friday without eating something too sugary.

In addition to this, try to reduce distractions and the pull from these apps. Deactivate notifications, because when we see one, we want to know what they are about, and the pull can be too difficult to resist. Social media notifications, for example, are usually tinged with red, and we want to click on them. Try to disable notifications and make your apps harder to access—for instance, uninstall Facebook or Instagram or Twitter from your phone; you could still access them via the browser, but it requires additional steps (Kohlbach, 2021, *How to Effectively Beat Social Media Distraction*).

Some authors have suggested turning your phone grayscale and removing the pretty colors that make a big part of the experience; this might be a good way for some to make their phone or computer less exciting for the time being, although it is more of a cosmetic solution. It can also reduce the appeal of many games or apps that rely on their visual appeal (Hern, 2017, *Will Turning Your Phone to Grayscale Really Do Wonders for Your Attention?*). You can also turn off the sound on your phone for games or apps, as notifications often come with a ping or a sound that draws your attention as well.

For social media, if it's something you need for work or use for specific purposes, like getting updates on family or friends, you can also go through all the accounts and content you follow to make sure it's aligned with your values and goals. Delete or stop following any account that is allowing you to waste time with memes or scroll down mindlessly; keep only the content you feel offers value to you, be it in the form of true enjoyment rather than just distraction, or learning, or socialization.

Get informed about how you are being manipulated

Many things are designed to trick us, to get us to spend our money and time on things that don't benefit us. Video game design, for example, often uses tricks or strategies that leave you engaged and wanting to spend money. Social media can exploit different vulnerabilities in your psyche to keep you scrolling.

When you become more aware of these practices, they can become easier to resist. Learn about the ethical quandaries of your favorite social media sites or games, especially if you find yourself drawn to them time and again. The goal is not to make you give up all social media or gaming, but to make more conscious choices and become aware when you are being manipulated against your own interests.

You have your own values that might conflict or align with the values that different corporations might represent. A conscious shift in consumption can involve the choice not to engage with the corporations that are doing harm according to your values. At the same time, you might find that this is not so easy to accomplish, as many companies play a pivotal role in our daily life and can be difficult to avoid. Still, mindful consumption can allow you to do better and help you feel like this aspect of your life is better aligned with your values and that you do things because you choose to, rather than falling for marketing schemes or ploys.

Better understanding how it happens can help you resist the related urges and respond differently to common triggers, like app notifications. It allows you to feel empowered in your interactions with social media rather than blindly follow the algorithm or let the app creators make choices for you.

Find other activities and introduce them into your day

It can be easy to fall for instant gratification when it's the most appealing option around. What if you have things that truly interest you and that attract you in different ways?

You can find new hobbies, new activities, new and novel tasks that will stimulate dopamine and allow you to develop better habits. Fill your day with interesting things that are more engaging and can make you feel more satisfaction. It could be time to pick up again that hobby you dropped for lack of time, or that art form that you have been eyeing for a while. Pick up new documentaries and courses, skills or crafts, toys, and activities that bring you pleasure.

Become more invested in planning and improving your leisure time. What are the things that truly appeal to you? Perhaps you enjoy nature or perhaps you are a big fan of new technologies. Maybe you might like cooking or drawing or sculpting with clay. Maybe there are some people you want to see more of.

When your day offers a lot of exciting and novel activities that you enjoy, it's easier to stay away from the meaningless ones. It also allows you to get your dopamine associated with achievement and propel your motivation to try and learn new things forward, creating a positive feedback loop.

Activities that are strongly associated with a positive sense of satisfaction and can make us forget all about our bad habits include socializing. Being around other people is more satisfying and rewarding, and our need to belong and share with others is compelling. Social activities, like meeting with friends or going to a reunion or participating in a class, can help us feel more motivated.

Novelty is another big factor. It engages our dopamine mechanisms because we are trying to guess whether we will like something, and it's fun to experience a new thing. Of course, if you expect to hate an activity, perhaps you will not be quite as excited. Still, if it surprises you, the feelings of reward you experience will be a lot stronger, but the disappointment if it indeed does not surprise you can demotivate you.

Finding positive activities, especially social ones and ones that take you outside the home, can make a big difference in what provides more dopamine for your brain. It allows you to learn new things and new perspectives that can facilitate habit change.

Take a trip

If all else fails, a trip to a novel area can help you reset your dopamine. It takes you out of your usual surroundings and brings you somewhere new, where there are limited triggers for negative behaviors and a lot of exciting experiences. Even a short trip can provide a nice shakeup for your mind and help you find a new perspective on your day-to-day life.

A trip is usually not enough on its own to make lasting changes to your habits, but it can provide a short space for you to reflect and consider the changes you want to make and what you would like to see more of in your life, and what type of experiences thrill you the most.

A trip doesn't need to be a week-long journey to another country. You can try exploring a nearby town. Even going to a part of your city you don't know can induce that novelty effect and allow you to explore, feeling like a tourist in a brand-new place.

Seek out novel sensations

Another way to achieve this is to seek out novel sensations. Plan to have at least a little novelty in your day; just a single experience that allows you to experience something you have not experienced before. It will help you train your brain to subsist on little and regular doses of dopamine rather than seek to cram a lot of stimulation into the brain.

New flavors and dishes, a new route from home to work or the other way around, a new smell for your dishwashing liquid—consider trying out things you never had before, and having sensory experiences that are not usual or customary.

When we get caught up in a routine, it becomes harder and harder to turn off our brain's autopilot. This has probably happened to you before. Say you were driving on your usual route and then arrived to find that you did not really remember the way there. Your brain was on autopilot.

You already know about mindfulness, which can serve as an antidote to this issue. But novelty is another option. It also helps your brain expect and anticipate novelty from simple things and improve dopamine production throughout the week.

You don't need to go on and try something wildly new and different. Just consider what type of sensory experience you might have. Try a new type of book or hobby, a movie of a genre you'd avoid most of the time, or anything else that comes to mind. Novelty can keep the brain happy and satisfied.

There are many things you can do to change the way in which your brain receives dopamine and how it motivates you. You can take control of your motivation and lifestyle to implement changes that will allow you to focus your time and efforts on positive, healthy habits.

It's worth remembering that dopamine has its positives and its negatives. We need it to function well and anticipate success and work toward achieving more. But many things in the modern world try to reroute our dopamine to serve their interests. Understanding how this chemical works and how we can use it more effectively can help us improve our lives in a measurable and direct way.

Your dopamine is an essential substance—it is called the "molecule of more" for a reason (Lieberman & Long, 2019, *The Molecule of More: How a Single Molecule in Your Brain Drives Love, Sex, and Creativity—and will Determine the Fate of the Human Race*). Dopamine is the chemical of striving for more and motivating ourselves. Without motivation, there is little that we can accomplish. By letting go of things that substitute genuine achievement and genuine success for less important and meaningful goals, you can build a life that is aligned with your values and that enables you to pursue things that truly matter—goals that are significant and purposeful and can make you feel like you are leaving your mark on the world.

Using the above strategies, you can effectively regulate your dopamine levels and reduce them consistently. Not only will you enjoy your life more because of it, but you will also enjoy life more regularly and find pleasure in meaningful, routine, and work activities. It will give you access to the control panel of your brain and allow you to pursue your true goals and achievements.

Summary

- Though dopamine is a natural part of the brain's chemistry, excessive levels can mimic addiction profiles, and hence a dopamine detox can help reset our brain to optimal levels, and allow us to experience challenge, reward and novelty in new, healthier ways.

- Detoxing involves reducing "easy" tasks that provide bursts of low-effort dopamine (such as social media, sugar, alcohol, shopping, or pornography) and replacing them with activities such as meditating, exercise, fasting, hobbies, reading, or sports.
- Feeling bored, deprived, frustrated, or even angry during a detox is normal, and a sign of how necessary a purge is! Persist with discomfort, however, and you will gradually recalibrate yourself. In time, you will train your brain to enjoy productive, healthy and gradual pleasures and accomplishments rather than instant gratification and distraction.
- Choose a 1-, 3-, or 7-day detox according to your needs, and work to rewire your brain and consider which behaviors you want to keep in your life, and which are harmful. By dialing down the thrills and instant gratification, you allow yourself the chance to think more deeply about your more authentic values and desires in life.
- A 7-day detox can be powerful, but needs some strategic planning ahead of time. Factor in plenty of opportunities for mindfulness and reflection, work with your boredom by anticipating it and choosing not to resist it, and focus on the process of what is happening with your cravings and your denial of those cravings.

- Good sleep habits, nutrition, and exercise are part and parcel of rewiring your brain. Liberally use awareness and relaxation techniques. The goal is not deprivation, but to rework your relationship to pleasure, action, and awareness. The goal is to gain conscious mastery and control over your own life and what you most want to create for yourself.

PART 2

The Food That Fuels Us

You are what you eat. Really, truly, and literally—every organ, tissue, molecule, and even atom that is inside your body has come from somewhere. Your food, every new neural connection you make, every movement your muscles bring about, and every hair on your head is a direct result of the nutrition you take in—or not. Furthermore, the food you eat affects your capacity to synthesize neurotransmitters like dopamine, which then influence every last inch of your subjective experience.

Proper nutrition may seem like a pretty boring way to start a book on revamping your life, but it's no exaggeration that if you want to build a better physical experience, you need to start with the foundation. Food does two powerful things: it supplies the energy you need to power every biological function that keeps you alive, and it also provides the raw materials that your body uses to repair and build itself. What could be more fundamental than that?

The food we eat has a huge impact on everything that we do, our energy levels, and our overall well-being. We have learned a lot more about nutrition in the past few decades, and yet there are many contradictory ideas and suggestions for improving your health. Just take a look at all the different diets that people pursue:

keto, paleo, or vegan, all of which present and promote themselves as the solution to all your problems and as a path to better health and a longer life, which make this topic of interest to the biohacking community.

In this section, we will discuss some tips and strategies associated with nutrition, try to make sense of current advice, and spend some time talking about probiotics and prebiotics and other modern strategies for improving your well-being by improving what you eat. We will also examine the most popular diets and the best takeaways we can glean from each of these, even if we choose not to diet or to diet in a different way.

CHAPTER 3

Fuel for Life

Nutrition is an ever-advancing science that offers new insights and new ideas about how to improve one's health through food. This also means, however, that some current information that is state-of-the-art might soon become outdated or debunked. This information is based on current trends and ideas and reflects the current understanding, but it's worth staying up to date with new findings and ideas about the topic in order to make the most informed choices.

Researcher Michael Pollan (2009, *Food Rules: An Eater's Manual*), who specializes in food and nutrition, has described the current approach to food with this simple set of rules:

"Eat food. Not too much. Mostly plants."

This means that we should consume primarily real food, and fewer processed products, or products with a complex content of chemicals, or artificial foods. This is how we can describe the first phrase. The second one refers to eating in moderation and with good balance, not consuming too much of any element, like carbs, fats, or even protein, and avoiding too-large portions or meals. Overindulgence is the second key thing to watch out for, and it's better to cut down portions for each meal rather than to consume too much and leave the table stuffed.

The third rule refers, of course, to increased consumption of fruit and vegetables, as this is guaranteed to provide better effects for one's health. While protein is also important, adding a lot of fruit and vegetables to each meal can make a huge difference to a person's diet (Pollan, 2009, *Food Rules: An Eater's Manual*).

Following more general principles, rather than rules that are stricter, can make you better able to control and manage your diet and stay healthier. Rules that feature very concrete principles, like not eating bread, tend to be more difficult to follow and restrictive; unless, of course, they have to do with allergies or medical conditions.

You can make changes in your diet to make it healthier without necessarily upending all your habits. Try to include more fruit and vegetables and products that are less processed and fresh. Fish, meat, chicken, and other similar products are better bought fresh and ready to be cooked than precooked.

Having more foods that you enjoy makes it easier to eat at home. Often, when we think of delicious foods, we first consider the processed, sweet, and salty options like chips, cookies, or chocolate. However, natural foods can be as delicious, especially if you take into account your own taste when preparing them. You are not obliged to eat salmon if you don't like salmon, or asparagus if you don't like asparagus. Home cooking also allows you to create desserts and snacks that are healthier than their store-bought options and can be enjoyed without guilt. Even desserts that are traditionally viewed as unhealthy can be nutritious and pleasant when made from the right ingredients.

Not everyone has the option to always cook at home, of course, or to access all the healthy foods available. Yet, consider how you can move closer to these ideal goals. Maybe you can't cook at home every day—but you can do it every Friday or twice a week. Maybe you don't have access to a lot of fresh vegetables, but you can get canned or frozen ones. It's not an easy road, but even small changes can make a big difference in how you feel and the habits that you create.

More plants, less food, and more "real" food help build a sustainable and healthy diet that can serve as the basis for an effective biohacking process. Having a healthy diet might not be as exciting as doing other practices or hacks, but it lays the foundation for a better and longer life alongside a healthy sleep schedule.

The Mediterranean diet

The Mediterranean diet is considered one of the most solid and established diets for the prevention of health issues and for longevity. It is considered a gold standard of preventive medicine thanks to all the evidence supporting its benefits and unique capacity to reduce the risks of myocardial infarction, stroke, mortality, heart failure, and disability; it also seems to lead to a better quality of life and greater life satisfaction (Martinez-Gonzalez & Martin-Calvo, 2016, *Mediterranean Diet and Life Expectancy; Beyond Olive Oil, Fruits, and Vegetables*). This diet has solid empirical support and seems to be one of the best options for people who want to eat healthy, live longer, and also support their cardiovascular health.

The Mediterranean diet is associated with countries near the Mediterranean, like Greece and Italy, and features many staples of the region. The Mediterranean diet is characterized by several key elements.

There are a lot of plant-based foods in this diet, including vegetables, fruits, nuts, legumes, and unprocessed cereals. It features low consumption of meat and meat products—especially low with regards to red meat and processed meats like sausages. There is a moderate to high consumption of fish and not a lot of dairy, with the exception of traditional yogurt and some types of cheese. Alcohol is part of this diet but is consumed in moderation and with meals. It involves wine rather than other forms of alcohol (Martinez-Gonzalez & Martin-Calvo, 2016, *Mediterranean Diet and Life Expectancy; Beyond Olive Oil, Fruits, and Vegetables*).

The Mediterranean diet is associated with a high consumption of fats, which make up about 40% of products consumed within this diet. Most fats, however, are healthy fats—in particular, olive oil. Most of the fats consumed here are beneficial monounsaturated lipids. Extra-virgin olive oil can make up around 10-

15% of total calorie content within this diet (Martinez-Gonzalez & Martin-Calvo, 2016, *Mediterranean Diet and Life Expectancy; Beyond Olive Oil, Fruits, and Vegetables*).

While the Mediterranean diet is made up of fats, it's mostly healthy fats. Healthy fats appear to protect the heart, as one of the main benefits of this diet is the prevention of heart issues. It seems that consuming and favoring olive oil over other sources of fat and for cooking and seasoning is a good takeaway, as is increasing the consumption of healthy fats over other types of foods.

The Okinawan diet

The Okinawan Diet is presented as a competitor with the Mediterranean diet. This is because it also is proving to sustain longevity. The two diets share some common patterns of eating, however, such as more seafood and an intake of healthy fats.

The Okinawan diet's staples are root vegetables (sweet potatoes), green and yellow vegetables, soybean-based foods, and medicinal plants. Marine foods and lean meats are consumed in moderation as a source of protein. There is a high intake of unrefined carbohydrates and healthy fats, and a moderate protein intake with fish, legumes, vegetables, and lean meats as sources (Willcox, Scapagnini, & Willcox, 2014, *Healthy Aging Diets Other Than the Mediterranean: A Focus on the Okinawan Diet*).

This Japanese diet is associated with a lower risk of cardiovascular diseases and other age-related conditions. It seems to lead to a higher well-being across the lifespan and reduce inflammation thanks to its fat profile (Willcox, Scapagnini, & Willcox, 2014, *Healthy Aging Diets Other Than the Mediterranean: A Focus on the Okinawan Diet*).

The main takeaway from this diet appears to be the benefits of protein sources that are not red or fatty meats; rather, lean meats, seafood, legumes, and vegetables seem to offer a better source. Healthy fats come up once again as an important factor for a healthy diet.

The keto diet

The keto diet has become popular in recent months, but the empirical support for this diet is less optimistic than for the Mediterranean diet. A keto diet is associated with drastically reducing carb intake and increasing the intake of fats. The staples of this diet are concentrated fats, meat, poultry, fish, eggs, and cheese. It reduces the consumption of fruits, legumes, whole grains, and some forms of vegetables or eliminates them outright (Crosby et al., 2021, *Ketogenic Diets and Chronic Disease: Weighing the Benefits Against the Risks*).

The keto, or ketogenic, diet is low on carbohydrates, modest on protein, and high on fat. The goal is to induce a state of ketosis, or production of ketone bodies, that serves as a source of energy and promotes the burning of fat. The keto diet appears to contribute to weight loss and has some benefits, such as a decrease in blood pressure and triglycerides. It also might lead to increased cardiovascular risks, however, and might be difficult to maintain over time (Batch, Lamsal, Adkins, Sultan, & Ramirez, 2020, *Advantages and Disadvantages of the Ketogenic Diet: A Review Article*).

The keto diet suggests eliminating fruits and reducing vegetables, which might not be advisable. A restrictive diet might benefit the person short-term, as it is hard to sustain over a long time. Though it reinforces the importance of healthy fats in the diet, there are some concerns over the amount of saturated fat that typically come with a diet heavy in red meat, eggs and fish. Finally, one downside of the keto diet is that while it promotes rapid fat loss, it is an environmentally unsustainable way of eating, and is practically impossible to follow for those wanting to avoid animal products.

The paleo diet

The paleo diet is based on the idea that we should eat more similarly to our Paleolithic-era ancestors, consuming products that people have eaten since the beginning of the species. This means eating mostly vegetables, fruits, nuts, roots, and meat (are you sensing the theme here?). It excludes dairy products, grains, sugars, legumes, processed oils, salt, alcohol, and coffee. Processed foods are to be avoided (Sachdev, Priya, & Gayathri, 2018, *Paleo Diet — A Review*). Paleo appears to lead to some health benefits, but, once more, the support is not as clear as it is for the Mediterranean diet.

Paleo appears to show positive effects for healthy, but no more than other healthy diets (Jamka et al., 2020, *The Effect of the Paleolithic Diet vs. Healthy Diets on Glucose and Insulin Homeostasis: A Systematic Review and Meta-Analysis of Randomized Controlled Trials*). In particular, a problem could be that this diet restricts important foods like legumes, grains, and dairy foods (Fenton & Fenton, 2016, *Paleo Diet Still Lacks Evidence*).

The paleo diet's strength is the focus on vegetables, fruit, and nuts, as well as avoidance of processed foods. People find eating this way restrictive and unsustainable, however, and as with any diet that excludes large food groups, there may be an exacerbation of eating disordered behaviors or anxiety around eating the "right" thing.

Diet tips would include:

- High level of intake of healthy fats
- Lean meats and fish rather than meat
- Vegetables and fruit
- Lower carbs and fewer processed foods

Superfoods and supplements

Superfoods tend to receive a lot of hype, but also come and go with fads. A superfood is a term that is used to describe a food with special and increased healthy properties that can contribute to a healthy diet on its own. To be classified as a superfood, a food needs to have a dozen or more properties that make it beneficial. In particular, it might have polyunsaturated fatty acids (omega-3 and 6), vitamins, minerals, probiotics, antioxidants, essential amino acids, enzymes, and more.

What are the advantages of superfoods? It's easier to reap the benefits of this type of food because the vitamins and other elements are absorbed naturally, so they can enhance nutrition. While no single superfood can cure all diseases on its own, they can serve as a good addition to diets and improve well-being and health.

What are some recognized superfoods? There are blueberries and raspberries, acai berries, pomegranates, walnuts and almonds, cocoa, sweet potatoes, mastic, broccoli, spinach, seaweed like spirulina, kefir, ginger, tea, and honey (Proestos, 2018, *Superfoods: Recent Data on Their Role in the Prevention of Diseases*).

Adding these superfoods can improve the diet by increasing the number of nutrients we consume. These can also fit into the diet and offer a host of benefits, in particular with regard to the antioxidants and vitamins they contain.

There are hundreds of different supplements out there. Some people swear by particular substances or brands, and biohackers also have their preferred options or specialized supplements that are meant to achieve specific goals. But what is the reality of supplements?

They are not perfect or able to solve any issues on their own. They can help you achieve specific goals and get enough nutrients, however, if your diet is lacking in specific substances and elements your body actually needs.

The modern understanding of supplements suggests that they should complement a healthy diet and are not enough on their own to guarantee that you are receiving enough. Supplements come in many different flavors and mixes, as well as in different formats, like pills, drinks, powders, and more.

It's important to watch out for supplements that promise too much. If something is sold and offered as the new miracle cure that will give you lots of energy, fix your health, and more, it's likely to be a fad or even a scam rather than a helpful option. In particular, watch out for pills that have a dubious place of origin or are not manufactured by a reliable company.

Supplements are not as regulated by official mechanisms such as the FDA, so these tend to only intervene when a supplement is doing serious harm. It's important to stick to reliable brands and known vitamin and nutrient names rather than plants or herbs or chemicals. Some pills can be ineffective, while others can be outright harmful. If you take medication, it's important to check each ingredient, as even natural herbs can interfere with the effects of your medication. For example, activated charcoal that has become a fashionable feature in many supplement products and healthy drinks can neutralize the effects of any medication (WebMD, 2021, *Activated Charcoal*).

Some supplements have a good and recognized history of being helpful. B12 can improve nerve health, folic acid is often taken during pregnancy, and people often have a vitamin D deficiency. Fish oil and omega supplements, among others, are well-understood and widely consumed. Some are often recommended for people with particular deficits or difficulties, but scientific evidence is not as clear for many others. In particular, the benefits of multivitamins are often questioned, especially in the long term and for people who eat a varied, well-rounded diet (The University of Utah, 2020, *Do Those Supplements Actually Work?*). It is clear that supplements won't fix diseases or actually make you live longer, but can improve your health in clear ways in the short term and also boost your energy.

Supplements are not always safe. Most do not cause any health problems and do not pose any risks, unless you exceed the recommended daily dosage. People with chronic conditions like liver disease, those on medication, and those who are pregnant should be cautious when choosing what to take. It's worth remembering also that not all supplements offer what's advertised, in particular when they make wide and excessive claims about their effectiveness. Some examples of supplements with harmful effects include St. John's wort, which can reduce the effectiveness of medications like antidepressants and birth control; gingko, which can make the blood thinner; vitamin K, which, in contrast, can impact the effectiveness of blood thinners; and some herbal supplements like kava, which might even damage your liver (Penn Medicine, 2020, *The Truth About Supplements: 5 Things You Should Know*). It's also important to be careful with fad supplements that become fashionable, as there is often not sufficient research conducted about their safety and efficacy; in the future, those supplements could turn out to have harmful effects on people.

Supplements require a lot of research before they are taken. One thing is clear, however: they cannot replace a good diet and should be used mainly as a form of support rather than as a main solution (Penn

Medicine, 2020, *The Truth About Supplements: 5 Things You Should Know*).

A good idea is to identify whether your diet fully supports your nutritional needs with regard to each vitamin. A doctor and some official tests can help with this and target the supplements that will do the most good.

Multivitamins with a broader effect can be a good choice, as they are unlikely to cause harmful effects. Measure their impact—write down how you feel each day as you take the supplement, before you take the supplement, and after you stop taking it. Some might have a placebo effect, but this tracking ensures that you don't put too much stock in the promises of each option.

So, are there supplements that are generally safe and useful to take?

Vitamin D can reduce the risk of cancer and can reduce inflammation overall, as well as increase strength and reduce frailty (Zhang et al., 2019, *Association Between Vitamin D Supplementation and Mortality: Systematic Review and Meta-analysis*; Halfon, Phan, & Teta, 2015, *Vitamin D: A Review on Its Effects on Muscle Strength, the Risk of Fall, and Frailty*).

Omega-3 supplementation is associated with better cardiovascular outcomes and improved cardiovascular outcomes (Khan et al., 2021, *Effect of Omega-3 Fatty Acids on Cardiovascular Outcomes: A Systematic Review and Meta-analysis*).

And are there supplements that are not as good?

A longitudinal study focusing on selenium and vitamin E found no benefit and saw an increased rate of prostate cancer in men taking these supplements (NIH, 2015, *Selenium and Vitamin E Cancer Prevention Trial (SELECT): Questions and Answers*). Beta-carotene and vitamin A also might contribute to cancer risks (Goodman et al, 2004, *The Beta-carotene and Retinol Efficacy Trial: Incidence of Lung Cancer and Cardiovascular Disease Mortality During 6-Year Follow-up After Stopping Beta-Carotene and Retinol Supplements*).

One particular type of support you can use to enhance your health with some stronger empirical evidence is probiotics and prebiotics.

Your gut biome—using probiotics and prebiotics

Finally, let's turn to an area of research that does in fact show a lot of promise. The human gut has been called the second brain, and scientists are now claiming that an enormous percentage of the body's immunity, mood, and even social behavior is rooted not in the brain but in the gut, where trillions of microbes are working in close symbiosis with you and one another. It's a natural place for an amateur biohacker to focus.

You certainly have heard of antibiotics—medication that kills off undesirable bacteria. Probiotics are solutions that introduce new bacteria into our bodies, specifically into the gut, to improve our gut biome. Prebiotics serve as food for the helpful bacteria within us.

The importance of the gut biome has been increasingly recognized over the past few years. We know that our gut is the host to a wide selection of cells, and also bacteria; there are over 100 trillion gut bacteria that serve an important function for the body. In particular, they can produce specific proteins, improve our glucose tolerance, help digestion, and even help our immune system. The gut microbiome serves many important functions, although some of these are not yet known. The ecosystem of the gut is complex and features millions, even billions of different microorganisms that play a significant role in our daily well-being (Pelton, N.D., *Biohacking Your Microbiome*).

The gut microbiome is essential in many functions. It allows the body to ferment non-digestible parts of the food, like fibers, which leads to the growth of specialist microbes that produce fatty acids and gasses. These are directly connected to our health outcomes. A healthy biome can lead to lower risks of atherosclerosis and of major adverse cardiovascular events and even type 2 diabetes (Valdes, Walter, Segal, & Spector, 2018, *Role of the Gut Microbiota in Nutrition and Health*).

Our gut bacteria appears to play an important role in the development of obesity, as many studies show that overweight and obese individuals have a low diversity in their guts. Introducing microbes from fat mice to non-fat mice makes them more likely to gain weight (Valdes, Walter, Segal, & Spector, 2018, *Role of the Gut Microbiota in Nutrition and Health*).

Low bacterial diversity also seems to contribute to inflammatory bowel disease, psoriatic arthritis, type 1 diabetes, atopic eczema, coeliac disease, and arterial stiffness. While it might not cause all these diseases, it might indicate a connection between overall health and a healthy gut microbiome (Valdes, Walter, Segal,

& Spector, 2018, *Role of the Gut Microbiota in Nutrition and Health*).

While it sounds anything but appealing, transplanting gut microbiota from a healthy person to someone with a lower diversity or a specific problem, like some infections, can improve outcomes (Valdes, Walter, Segal, & Spector, 2018, *Role of the Gut Microbiota in Nutrition and Health*)

The gut microbiota is influenced by a variety of foods and practices. For instance, gut microbiota can be negatively affected by sugar substitutes like sucralose (Valdes, Walter, Segal, & Spector, 2018, *Role of the Gut Microbiota in Nutrition and Health*). Our understanding of gut microbes, though, is still quite limited and growing every year as more researchers become interested in the topic and more information about its importance becomes apparent.

All this means that if we can have more healthy and helpful bacteria in the gut and stimulate its functioning, we could improve our health significantly and even achieve positive results for different aspects of our body's well-being. Here is where probiotics and prebiotics come in.

Probiotic is a term that refers to live microbial or microorganism supplements that can help improve the host's well-being. Probiotics are, basically, a live colony of good bacteria that we eat and add to our internal microbiome. People who have been taking antibiotics, for example, might need to repopulate their guts, as the medication might have killed off some helpful bacteria alongside the harmful bacteria (Kechagia,

Basoulis, Konstantopoulou, Dimitriadi, Gyftopoulou, Skarmoutsou, & Fakiri, 2013, *Health Benefits of Probiotics: A Review*).

A prebiotic, on the other hand, is a good supplement or a food substance that is fed to the bacteria and stimulates specific types of growth or activity among the microorganisms. Prebiotics are not absorbed by our guts, but instead are processed by the bacteria. Simply put, prebiotics encapsulate everything we think of as fiber (and yes, there are many types of fiber!). We can consider them as a type of food for our gut microbiome that stimulates their working in our favor; i.e., we feed and support them, and they help us digest our food and modulate the production of certain hormones and neurotransmitters, for example (Kechagia, Basoulis, Konstantopoulou, Dimitriadi, Gyftopoulou, Skarmoutsou, & Fakiri, 2013, *Health Benefits of Probiotics: A Review*).

Some common types of probiotics include lactic acid bacteria, like Lactococcus and Bifidobacterium. These are often included in dairy products and are very good for our gut health (Kechagia, Basoulis, Konstantopoulou, Dimitriadi, Gyftopoulou, Skarmoutsou, & Fakiri, 2013, *Health Benefits of Probiotics: A Review*).

Including probiotics in our daily diet is important for nutrition and can also lead to health benefits. They appear to have some positive effects in preventing some problems with health and also improving conditions with other issues. In particular, probiotics can help with lactose intolerance, the side effects of antibiotics, diarrhea, allergies, and more. Probiotics are widely offered as supplements and also as a part of many dairy products, like yogurts, which makes them easy to consume and deliver. Probiotics have some good empirical support that suggests that taking one dose of probiotics per day can help us improve our well-being. Supplements and probiotic-rich foods like dairy products are accessible and can do a lot to improve the gut microbiome (Kechagia, Basoulis, Konstantopoulou, Dimitriadi, Gyftopoulou, Skarmoutsou, & Fakiri, 2013, *Health Benefits of Probiotics: A Review*).

Are there some exceptions to the rule? Yes. In general, it is not recommended that a person with an active bacterial infection consumes probiotics, nor is it a great idea to take them while also taking antibiotics. Instead, you can wait to finish the treatment and increase the use of probiotics to restore your gut microbiome. Also, look for trustworthy and reliable brands if you choose to take them as supplements.

Prebiotics, on the other hand, are food ingredients that promote beneficial growth. In essence, they are non-digestible by humans, but are good for bacteria and arrive at the colon without getting digested. Prebiotics usually come from foods, in particular fermented foods and others like garlic, onions, jicama, yogurts, kefir, sauerkraut, and more (Pelton, N.D., *Biohacking Your Microbiome*).

Some prebiotics are oligosaccharides, which can be found in carb-rich foods, like carrots, sweet potatoes, squash, and asparagus. They can also occur naturally in starches, like banana or plantain flour and raw potato starch (Pelton, N.D., *Biohacking Your Microbiome*).

Consuming foods that contain prebiotics is good for our health and can stimulate activity for our gut bacteria. A good tip is to have at least one product per day that is rich in prebiotics and that you can enjoy. Other than that, an excellent strategy is to fill your plate with a rich and varied array of different fruits, vegetables, and whole grains to supply the fiber and prebiotics necessary to support your gut bacteria. Probiotics and prebiotics potentiate each other and allow us to get the maximum benefits.

Probiotics and prebiotics are relatively easy to consume, as they are part of many different foods, including vegetables, fruit, fermented products, and dairy products. Supplements are available and can be found in many different packages and delivery options. There is a solid evidence base in favor of taking probiotics and prebiotics (Markowiak, & Śliżewska, 2017, *Effects of Probiotics, Prebiotics, and Synbiotics on Human Health*).

Summary

- Though nutrition science is always advancing and changing, we do know that good food is essential for a good life, and that the ideal human diet broadly follows Michael Pollan's nutrition rule: "Eat real food. Not too much. Mostly plants."
- Flexibility is key: rigid rules are unsustainable.
- There are countless diet philosophies out there; for example, the Mediterranean diet (plant-based and low meat, but heavily featuring

olive oil and moderation) the Okinawan diet (lean seafood protein, starchy plants, and good fats), and the keto diet (emphasis on low carb, high protein, and high fat eating that induces ketogenesis in the body).

- No single food is a miracle cure, but there are certain "superfoods" that are especially nutritious, such as broccoli or blueberries.
- Supplements, too, can boost a diet, although not all supplements are created equal, and no supplement is a replacement for a healthy diet. Since supplements are not FDA regulated, it's up to you to do your research. It's best to tailor your supplement use to fit your unique diet and lifestyle.
- There is increasing evidence for the beneficial use of probiotics and prebiotics (which is essentially the fiber that probiotics feed on).
- Probiotics can correct imbalances in the body's all-important gut microbiome, the health of which has far-reaching effects on every part of your body, including your weight and overall mental health. Though available in supplement form, it's best to get probiotic cultures into your diet naturally, with fermented foods such as kefir, yogurt, or kimchi. In addition, plenty of plant fiber and a diet low in sugar and alcohol will support a healthy gut bacterial balance.

CHAPTER 4

Nudging Your Nutrition

Overall, nutrition is complex. We can eat foods with complex ingredients and effects. Our own genetic makeup, preferences, and traditions can shape the way in which we eat and what works best for us. If you fall down the nutrition rabbit hole, you may soon find yourself getting overwhelmed by the enormous variety of opinions out there, and stress over the finer details.

But although nutrition is a complicated affair within the body, it doesn't have to be complicated on a day-to-day basis every time we put something in our mouths. In fact, the healthiest diet is often one that is natural, intuitive and low-stress. We don't need to spend enormous amounts of money on artificial supplements and books teaching bizarre regimes to effectively upgrade our nutrition. There are some general tips that can help you construct a healthy baseline diet, and these are not, in fact, complex. For instance, you should include plenty of plants in your diet and not eat in excess, no matter what you eat. No Ph.D. in chemistry required!

A good tip is to be mindful of supplements and consult with a doctor before using one, especially if you are taking medication or facing health issues. Supplements serve as a complement to a good diet but can help you compensate for some deficits. The easiest way to identify these deficits is to run blood tests. The principle is obvious: you make the most impact by identifying clear areas of deficit and targeting those first. For example, it would be useless to fine tune your intake of micronutrients and obscure minerals if you are consistently eating less fiber every day than you need. While people can get carried away optimizing fine details in their diets, the truth is that most of us could benefit from addressing the low hanging fruit first: 95% of your health and well-being comes from simple (and boring!) habits like eating enough fruit and vegetables, and seldom being in a caloric excess.

A Mediterranean or Okinawan diet seems to give the best results overall for promoting health and longevity, and one of its virtues is its flexibility. Try to integrate specific principles from these two diets even if you don't adhere to them, like eating more vegetables and plant-based foods, fewer processed meats, and more healthy fats. Forget about perfection and instead try to hit the mark at least 80% of the time.

Not every food has to be nutritious. On the other hand, you can add some superfoods to your meals—many of which are actually delicious anyway. Some are easy to get, like blueberries or walnuts, while others might be more challenging. Eating more superfoods can increase your vitamin and mineral intake, as well as an antioxidant effect on your body.

For supplements, vitamin D and omega-3 supplementation appears to be especially useful. But a healthy diet is fundamental for your well-being.

Mastering environmental nudges and micro-resolutions

Be honest—a lot of what you've just read is information you probably already know, right? And yet, chances are that you haven't implemented many of these strategies into your daily life. Sometimes, we *know* exactly what we need in our life to be better. We need to go to bed sooner, eat better, spend less money, or exercise. These solutions seem to be a short way away, but still unreachable.

This is why a big part of everyday biohacking is being aware of the behavioral and psychological components of behavioral change. As you're probably well aware, knowing what the right thing is and doing it are two different things. In essence, change comes from three separate factors: knowing that we need to change, knowing what we need to do to change, and then taking concrete action to make that change real. Without all three, our development is merely a wish, or something theoretical.

Luckily for us, there are countless small changes we can make to reach our chosen goals and cultivate our desired habits. We will talk about two powerful tools based on tiny, manageable changes: environmental nudges and micro-resolutions. While the previous section is all about the *why* and *what* of nutritional biohacking, the following section is about the *how.*

Nudge theory comes from behavioral economics and suggests that we can make people more likely to make specific choices by making small changes in their environment. We are not restricting their choices or taking them away; however, we are making people more inclined to take a particular path. Marketers do it all the time: why do you think the candy bars are right by the checkout lane? We can also use nudges in order to make better decisions in our daily life without having to invest a lot of effort. A well-implemented nudge makes the right choice easier.

A nudge is, then, a small feature in an environment that can alter our behavior in a positive or negative way. Nudges can be used for evil, too, but if you are applying this theory to yourself, you will probably pick a worthy goal.

Nudges are associated with the concept of choice architecture—arranging and designing the environment in a way that promotes specific choices. Every aspect of design is a choice. Think, for example, of a menu: the way in which the foods are presented and arranged can impact the choices the consumer makes. When you walk around a store or a mall, you are walking between choices, whether they were implemented well or not.

Choice architecture features six main elements. The first one is incentives. These suggest that the right incentive can make a person more inclined to particular choices. If this product includes a free gift, maybe you would choose it instead. In your personal life, you can provide your own incentives, which can be psychological as well as material.

The second element is mapping. Map out each choice to truly understand its benefits and downsides, and the hidden and upfront costs you are paying. For instance, if you choose to order a burger instead of a salad, you might be paying a long-term penalty of worse cardiovascular health, or indigestion later on. Allow yourself to consider everything involved in a choice.

The third element is defaults. A default is what happens when you do nothing to change it. What is your default? Is it the burger or the salad? Is it going out to exercise or staying in to sleep? Identify the default for the choice you want to change.

The next element is feedback. Feedback helps recognize what you are doing and whether it is working. How will you know that your choice was better? How will you know whether you have met your goals? What type of feedback will you receive from your environment, yourself, and others? (Groenwegen, 2021, *Nudging Explained*)

Next, you should expect errors. People make mistakes, and so will you. It's normal to fall off the wagon. Consider what you can do to reduce the likelihood of a bad choice and what you can implement to deal with the consequences.

Another consideration is that you should simplify complex choices. Imagine that you decide to do something productive with your evening instead of spending it watching Netflix. But what does it mean to be productive? Should you clean your house? Should you be creative and work on your great novel project instead? This is a complex choice that makes you more likely to simply plop down and watch TV. You might decide on particular activities for each free evening to make the choice once and for all, or leave your art supplies out to sit and get started right away.

Environmental nudges are not miraculous, but they can help you make the right choices easier. Often, they involve a small shift that is easy to make or needs to be only implemented once.

Next, we will consider some nudges you can create in your environment for more and better productivity and a healthier lifestyle.

Encouraging healthier eating

The first nudge is to limit access to unhealthy foods. Don't buy them, store them out of sight, or keep them out of your daily path. Put them on your top shelf or behind other products.

Instead, make healthier foods accessible. Place a fruit platter on the counter, or a vase with apples on your way from the bedroom to the office or the kitchen. Make sure everything is ready to eat. Keep water by your workspace to drink more water every day, or leave a glass with water out for the morning and the evening, so that you can drink it in one gulp without even thinking about it.

Throw out takeout menus (if you are old-fashioned) and delete food delivery apps from your phone. Keep a list of all the fruit or vegetables you intend to buy and replenish the stocks whenever you go to the shop.

Steer clear from the supermarket aisles that have products you don't want to buy. Follow your shopping list strictly and avoid the things you know will tempt you. Schedule your grocery shopping for after dinner. Add your Mediterranean products to the list and have them ordered automatically.

Consider your goal and the environmental cues that influence the fact that it is not getting done. If you want to stop eating chocolate, don't keep chocolate close by, for instance; hide it and keep some healthier snacks prepared instead.

Exercise

For exercise, consider leaving your exercise gear out and in the way, so that you can't ignore it or put it away. If you are often tempted by the couch, put stuff on the couch that you would have to remove before sitting down. Even better, put your exercise gear there to make sure you have to engage with it.

Add little bursts of exercise to your day—walk instead of taking the stairs, for instance, and make it easier by telling people around you what you intend to do, so that they might call you out when you don't actually do them. Invite your coworkers, friends, and family members to do them with you—it's more fun and offers to make it into a competition, for added motivation. Others might even remind you of these small exercise bursts when you would not remember otherwise.

The goal is to make your environment friendlier towards your goal of exercising in a particular way. Clear out a space and a time and leave reminders for yourself in that space. Make situations where doing the thing is easier than not doing the thing, where the exercise is right there and easy to access.

When applied to biohacking, nudge theory can help you implement better and healthier habits in eating, taking supplements, exercising, or using specific solutions. It can make your environment an ally for changing your body and enhancing your health, which is important at the start of the journey. When you are still tempted by sugars or unhealthy products or trying to stick to a diet, build an environment that supports good choices, and the change will be a lot more painless.

Micro-resolutions: tiny changes for big impacts

A micro-resolution is a concept from Caroline Arnold who defines it as a limited, specific, and measurable change that produces an immediate and observable benefit. It is a small and specific behavioral shift that makes a big difference, but is relatively easy to follow through on. It is targeted and focused, like a scalpel that is used to make a precise incision and influence the behavior that most needs a change (Arnold, 2014, *Small Move, Big Change: Using Micro-resolutions to Transform Your Life Permanently*).

The idea of a micro-resolution is similar to that of a nudge in the sense that it focuses on manageable and achievable change right now rather than on huge goals that often fall through. If you decide that you will shift your life come Monday—no more drinking or smoking or partying—you are setting yourself up for failure. It's a huge change, and you are not prepared to make it just willy-nilly. A micro-resolution is much more likely to succeed than a huge goal, and although the decision might be small, it sets you up for success and allows you to see a difference (Arnold, 2014, *Small Move, Big Change: Using Micro-resolutions to Transform Your Life Permanently*).

Many people have the goal of going on a diet to lose weight. Most of them do not maintain this diet and fail in their ultimate goal. Yet, a micro-resolution makes you primed for success. In this case, you could consider what is contributing most to your weight or unhealthy nutritional habits. Maybe you eat a big chocolate bar every day or drink a beer in the evenings. Perhaps you could trade the big chocolate bar for a small one, or the beer for half a beer. If you are used to eating snacks while you watch TV, you could switch from buttered popcorn to low-calorie popcorn. The goal is to find something that scratches the same itch but is better for you in the long run (Arnold, 2014, *Small Move, Big Change: Using Micro-resolutions to Transform Your Life Permanently*).

Would it be better to, perhaps, decide to never eat chocolate ever again? Or less dramatically, to stop eating chocolate every day and eat a bar on the weekends? Perhaps. But that is the type of goal you are less likely to meet. The chocolate serves a function—maybe you want to treat yourself to something sweet after a long, hard day, and giving it up would leave you feeling dissatisfied and with cravings. Maybe you could try to stop snacking during TV time altogether, but find that you don't enjoy it. When you let go of a habit cold turkey, it leaves behind an empty space that wants to be filled, and the most common outcome is to go back to the habit, defeated and unmotivated (Arnold, 2014, *Small Move, Big Change: Using Micro-resolutions to Transform Your Life Permanently*).

A micro-resolution is easy to keep, though. It's easy to buy a bag of small candy bars that might mean that you reduce your calorie intake for that snack by half or more. You still get your craving and your sweet treat, but there is likely to be a significant impact (Arnold, 2014, *Small Move, Big Change: Using Micro-resolutions to Transform Your Life Permanently*).

If we connect it to the theme of biohacking, consider the biggest impacts. Maybe you have never stuck to taking pills for a while—a resolution could be to add a multivitamin to your meals once a day. It won't be a huge change, but you might start noticing the benefits and motivate yourself to move on to taking more supplements. Or instead, perhaps, you could get a superfood you enjoy and add it to your breakfast; for example, eating blueberries with your morning oatmeal. It's a small change with strong potential impacts.

Setting a micro-resolution requires some planning and thinking. Consider the habits that might be susceptible to change and are likely to leave a big impact.

It's a good idea to target things you do often and that are likely to have repercussions. If you consume 500 extra calories every day, cutting them down in half to 250 makes a change and leaves an impact.

The key to using this technique is to think small, but strategically. Do not try to make a micro-resolution that involves a big shift—the idea is to make it easy, almost natural, but consistent (Arnold, 2014, *Small Move, Big Change: Using Micro-resolutions to Transform Your Life Permanently*).

The keys to setting micro-resolutions involve focusing on one specific, small, achievable thing. Don't set the resolution as the goal of running every day. Decide that you will walk between your car and your office rather than use the elevator to go up and down (Arnold, 2014, *Small Move, Big Change: Using Micro-resolutions to Transform Your Life Permanently*).

Identify the target behavior and set a specific resolution. Avoid any resolutions that use words like never, always, every time, every day, absolutely, etc., or that imply those words or something similar. Focus on specific behaviors in specific situations—I won't order dessert in restaurants (but can still order it at a café or buy it for home), I will use the stairs in the office (but can take the elevator in other buildings or situations), I will eat a Mediterranean-style meal once a week, or add one dish to my regular menu, or even just learn to cook fish in a way that appeals to me (Arnold, 2014, *Small Move, Big Change: Using Micro-resolutions to Transform Your Life Permanently*).

Micro-resolutions target a specific issue with our behavior—our desire to do more and better and make huge sweeping changes. We tend to overestimate our ability to make behavioral shifts and, even if we fail, we rarely learn from experience. Micro-resolutions are almost certain to succeed and lead to changes. Later, we can make other micro-resolutions, chipping away at the habits we would like to modify (Arnold, 2014, *Small Move, Big Change: Using Micro-resolutions to Transform Your Life Permanently*).

Light and temperature

Our bodies are influenced by many different factors, from what we eat to how we sleep. There are, however, two factors that can impact our biological rhythms, our well-being, and offer new options for biohacking. They are the often-ignored light and temperature.

Let's start with light. We often take it for granted, especially as most homes, by far, have access to artificial lighting. But natural light and artificial light can influence our body's rhythms, moods, and even some aspects of our mental health.

The first function of light is to signal to our brains when it's time to go to bed (because darkness is coming and the light dims) and when it's time for our day's work (because the light is bright). Even though we have had lightbulbs for a while, this is still the same. Exposure to bright light before bed can make it harder for us to fall asleep, as it disrupts the release of melatonin, a hormone that promotes sleepiness.

When we don't get enough light in the mornings, we can remain groggy. It's much harder to wake up and do stuff when the world is still dark, and that has a physiological basis, too. Light is the number one factor that helps our body decide whether it's time to be up and about or sleeping, which can have significant effects on our ability to stay alert, to fall asleep, and to feel awake or tired when it's consistent with our biological rhythms.

An unexpected effect of light is that it can contribute to our mental health. People who live in countries with a marked loss of natural light in fall and winter are often subject to a problem known as seasonal affective disorder, or SAD—a type of depression that is linked to a lack of sunlight. It is treated by exposure to sunlight or to lamps that simulate sunlight. But even if you are not subject to this problem, sunlight exposure, even for 30 minutes a day (and even if it is cloudy out), makes a big difference with regard to our mood and mental health, as it supports the release of serotonin, which serves a variety of different functions inside the brain (APA, 2013, *The Diagnostic and Statistical Manual of Mental Disorders*; Kotz, 2007, *Get Healthier and Happier*).

Natural light is good for us, and it's important to be exposed to it in the morning and avoid it in the evening and the night; but even artificial light can do in a pinch. There are some modern controversial ideas about light and how else it can be used for therapeutic purposes.

Red light therapy is a controversial treatment approach that has been in use since the 90's. It involves exposing the skin or parts of the skin to red light at low frequencies in order to promote healing, boost the immune system, and help fight different skin problems as well. It can also be used to treat seasonal affective disorder. The evidence at the moment is mixed, but these practices are used in different clinics (Cobb, 2020, *Red Light Therapy Benefits*).

In addition to red light therapy, there is blue light therapy that can be used for repairing sun damage to the skin and even for some cancerous growths. It can be used for treating acne (using several sessions) and also employed for seasonal affective disorder (Cobb & Gotter, 2017, *Blue Light Therapy*).

This suggests that light has some healing properties, although its use is limited and it needs to be done carefully. You can't just go out into the sun for hours—it might lead to more skin damage. But it does not appear like light, beyond natural light and sleep management, is as effective for biohacking. Light-based treatments tend to focus on specific conditions, like acne, sun damage, and more.

Understanding how light affects our mood and biological rhythms, though, is important, as it allows us to have an easy way to boost our mood and to control and regulate our sleep successfully.

It's good to have at least half an hour of light exposure every day, and natural light seems to work best. Natural light in the morning and early afternoon can lead to better results.

What about temperature? We can use temperature to regulate our bodies, and there are some ideas that increased temperatures and reduced temperatures can serve health functions.

Temperature can affect how easy or hard it is for us to sleep. It's best to keep the room cool to help reduce our body's temperature, which is a natural process when we fall asleep. By keeping the temperature around 68 degrees Fahrenheit or 20 degrees Celsius, you promote a healthy rest. It can be hard to sleep in a hot and stuffy room, but also in a room that is too cold.

Cold exposure is used by many athletes to increase their power and add another layer of difficulty to their workout sessions. By lowering your temperature before a workout (for example, by drinking cold water) or doing the workout in a cool space or outdoors in winter, you can challenge your body more but also amplify your performance. Cold is also used to reduce soreness and swelling after an injury, with some athletes using ice baths to recover and get back into the game faster. Cryotherapy or full-body cold exposure in specially designed rooms is also becoming quite popular, but the benefits here are not fully based on science (Shmerling, 2018, *Cryotherapy: Can It Stop Your Pain Cold?*).

You can use the power of cold to enhance your athletic performance and recover after an injury by applying cold to the affected area. Cold showers can even boost your mood, not just your physical well-being, and exposure to cold water and temperatures without going to extremes might be another way to get your spirits up. It's worth noting that you should be careful when doing cold exposure in the wild, when it's an extreme temperature, or when you have some pre-existing conditions that could make cold dangerous. Cold can cause burns and damage the skin, as well as put more strain on your body (Shmerling, 2018, *Cryotherapy: Can It Stop Your Pain Cold?*; Asprey, N.D., *Your Thermostat May Be Key to Burning More Calories and Getting Focused*).

What about the heat? Hot environments can also put more strain on your body and make your workout more effective. Hot environments like saunas and similar can also bring your mood up. Being in a hot space can be tiring, too, and strain your body, however, so know your limits and don't overdo it with the temperature, or you might end up dehydrated (Asprey, N.D., *Your Thermostat May Be Key to Burning More Calories and Getting Focused*).

Both heat and cold can make you spend a lot more energy on doing your daily tasks or exercising, which can promote weight loss more than just having physical activity. It is important to remember that it strains the body more, and it's especially important to have water at hand and to keep to one's limits to avoid injury (Asprey, N.D., *Your Thermostat May Be Key to Burning More Calories and Getting Focused*).

Hot environments also bring down our cognitive performance. We can do better in a cool room—not too cold and not too hot, either. Warm rooms can make us more relaxed and less focused, but too much cold can make us distracted because of our chattering teeth (Asprey, N.D., *Your Thermostat May Be Key to Burning More Calories and Getting Focused*).

Heat and cold can stimulate our bodies in different ways. It can also depend on our individual preferences and tolerance and habits. Some people are sensitive to cold, and others to heat. Some feel they can't work when it's too warm, while others might struggle to motivate themselves moving in a low temperature. This means that you should also be mindful of your own state and well-being. Pushing yourself too hard can lead to health problems, as something like extreme cold or heat might make you sick or leave you with more issues. Take it step by step—don't try jumping into icy water or going to an extreme sauna.

If you are feeling like your workout is stagnating and not giving you enough benefits, if you struggle to sleep, if you are dealing with pain or want to maximize your focus—try playing around with the temperature where you are and see how your state changes when the thermostat does.

It's easy enough to take advantage of the properties of temperature and light. You can have lights that dim or become brighter or, at least, have alternative sources of light for the evening that use a red, warmer light that imitates the natural sunset.

Cold and hot showers are the easiest options for raising and lowering your body temperature. Experiment with these showers in the morning and the evening, before and after doing a workout, and see how your body responds.

Cryotherapy is an option for those interested in exploring the properties of full-body cold exposure. You can try an ice bath instead or seek a reliable place for cryotherapy near you. More focused applications of cold can help you relieve pain and soreness, too.

There are many things you can do to hack your body to enhance performance, improve your health and well-being, and boost every aspect of your life. Make sure to focus on hacks that are better proven and avoid those that are still suspicious. Always experiment and see what works for you and what brings the best results with regards to the efforts. You can discover your own personal hacks and create a stable routine that takes you closer to your goals.

Summary

- Though we all know the principles of a healthy diet, cultivating good habits takes time and effort.
- "Nudge theory" is all about the small changes we can make to our environment that will prompt the desired behavior. Everything is a choice, but we can make the right choice easier and more automatic by tweaking the environment.
- Ensure that there is always a feedback mechanism in place for any behavior, and try to simplify complex behaviors and choices as much as possible. Examples of nudges include keeping snack foods in the house, avoiding tempting aisles in the grocery store, or connecting exercise to other, more established habits in your routine. Done right, a nudge helps you do the right thing without expending too much extra willpower!
- Caroline Arnold's concept of micro-resolutions tells us that big things are possible when we commit to tiny steps. If you make a small but

specific change in the right direction and *stick to it*, the cumulative effect can be immense.

- To make a micro-resolution, identify a target behavior, then make tiny commitments toward change, avoiding anything dramatic or extreme. Think small but think strategically—make the smallest change you know you can stick with indefinitely.
- Two factors we know influence our eating behavior are light and temperature. Working with our biological rhythms is easier than working against them, and is more likely to lead to sustainable and healthful changes.
- At the bare minimum, expose yourself to natural light on waking in the morning, and avoid artificial light late into the night. Similarly, heat and cold can be used to wake the body up or encourage the natural signals to sleep.

PART 3

Sleeping Your Way to the Top

In our quest to master and elevate our biology, we have considered the uber-neurochemical dopamine, as well as the effect of nutrition. And now, we consider the final piece in the trio: sleep. The term bio-"hacking" has obvious programming and computer science origins, but the truth is that the human body is not at all like a machine. It is made of living components that will, even in the best-case scenario, degrade and die in time. It also does something that machines don't need to do: rest. The body is an organism that alternates between periods of energy expenditure and periods of recuperation, recovery, and regeneration. It is capable of growth and expansion, but to do so, it requires periods of relative inactivity where it goes dormant and simply rests.

Therefore, to work closely with our own biology and make it the best it can be, we need to respect this natural need for "down time" and use it to our advantage. This makes sleep one of the most important areas to biohack. You might have seen controversial articles about tricking your body into thriving on 3 hours of sleep a night, or running marathons in a fasted state, but the less glamorous truth is that a healthy, vibrant body is not a superhuman machine, but an animal with limitations that need to be respected.

CHAPTER 5

The True Importance of Sleep

Sleep is, without exaggeration, the most important requirement for your health. You can go without food and water for days, and your body can happily survive for years without supplements or medicine. But ask it to go without sleep for just a few days and the cracks will show.

Does sleep improve physical health? Absolutely. Emotional health? Even more so. It can improve our relationships, our creativity, our problem-solving capacity, and many other things. While sleep is not always valued in society, more and more evidence suggests that it is one of the fundamental elements for our well-being. Here's a hint: biohacking our sleep schedule is less about doing without sleep, and more about finding ways to put sleep back in its rightful place.

Sleep is neglected in society. Hustle culture suggests that we should be working as much as possible and pushing ourselves to our limits. Many workplaces interrupt the leisure time of employees, and some people consider sleep a liability. But research from the last few years shows without a doubt the power that sleep has and just how much it impacts your health (Walker, 2018, *Why We Sleep*).

What happens if we don't sleep? It would be easier to list everything that is not negatively affected by sleep rather than what is! Research suggests that for most adults, teens, and kids, sleep deprivation leads to ongoing short-term and long-term effects.

Without sleep, you will have reduced attention and memory capacity. We will react slower: our motor skills will be sluggish and the times that we take to respond increase. Sleep deprivation leads to accidents in the workplace and at home, and contributes to car accidents, being one of the leading causes of dangerous situations on the road (Gottlieb, Ellenbogen, Bianchi, & Czeisler, 2018, *Sleep Deficiency and Motor Vehicle Crash Risk in the General Population: A Prospective Cohort Study*).

Our mood shifts. We are more irritable and more prone to all types of negative emotions in general. It's easier to snap and lash out at others, hurting our relationships.

Sleep deprivation is associated with low energy and productivity. We can't do as much and what we can do tends to take longer. It hurts creativity and problem solving.

With regard to mental health, sleep deprivation contributes to depression and anxiety, as well as other issues. Without enough sleep, we have a bigger risk of developing type 2 diabetes, high blood pressure, heart disease, stroke, and even early death. When we don't sleep, we tend to eat more and eat less healthy foods, which can also make us more likely to be obese. It harms the immune system and makes us more likely to catch an illness. Children and teens who don't sleep enough have more issues with their growth and development (Babson, Trainor, Feldman, & Blumenthal, 2010, *A Test of the Effects of Acute Sleep Deprivation on General and Specific Self-reported Anxiety and Depressive Symptoms: An Experimental Extension*).

We might not always recognize the effects of sleep deprivation. If it becomes a chronic problem (which is common for most adults across the world), we might perceive this state as our new normal. It becomes the benchmark by which we measure ourselves, even though better sleep quality could change what we do and how we feel. A risk of sleep deprivation is that we start experiencing microsleeps. Microsleep is, essentially, a short period of time when your brain shuts down. You will often not be aware of what is happening, but you might miss your daily experiences. If it happens while you are driving or engaged in another thing that requires you to be alert, it can be quite dangerous. We can't stop ourselves from experiencing microsleep (Kennedy, Howard, & Pierce, 2001, *Microsleep Literature Review*).

Often, you might feel that you are fine, or just a bit drowsy. But that doesn't mean that you are judging your state accurately. More often than not, we will overestimate our ability to do well when lacking sleep.

Here are just some of the risks a person with chronic sleep deprivation faces throughout their day. They might:

- Make a costly mistake at work by forgetting about an important project
- Crash a car
- Get into a fight with their loved ones
- Fail to exercise or eat healthy
- Fail to recognize the solution to a problem they are facing
- Cut themselves with a kitchen knife by accident
- Trip and fall
- Spend the day feeling poorly, tired, or unmotivated
- Catch a nasty cold

Sleep is essential to get our brain working and feeling properly. Our 7 to 9 hours of sleep can help us be alert and improve our learning. We can memorize things and remember them better. Our mood improves, and we are more creative. We operate at the top of our game.

A good night's rest helps us regulate emotions and reduces the risks we face of having an accident. It boosts our motivation and productivity. Sleep can improve our physical, emotional, and mental health.

Current research strongly supports the idea that the lack of sleep we are experiencing hits us where it hurts the most (Walker, 2018, *Why We Sleep*). Indeed, it hits us pretty much evenly, hurting our bodies, brains, emotions, and minds. It keeps us from living up to our potential. We might not always even be aware of the damage it is doing. If you are one of those people who lives a clean lifestyle, exercises frequently, eats their veggies, and says mantras in the mirror every morning, it might be sobering to realize that you could be undoing every ounce of hard work by getting fewer hours of sleep every night than you need.

Circadian rhythms

This establishes the huge importance sleep has and justifies the need to work on making sleep quality better. But in order to understand how we can improve our sleep quality, we need to go over an important concept.

> *Circadian rhythms—the changes in our bodies and minds that follow a 24-hour cycle.*

A major underlying theme in everyday biohacking is to work with what our bodies are already designed to do. While more extreme biohackers like to experiment with how far they can push our natural capacities, and how they can redesign human organisms from the ground up, more conventional wisdom knows that the greatest opportunities for development lie, paradoxically, in our ability to be more of what we are, not less.

Circadian rhythms are a key example of the deep, ingrained habits our bodies have evolved over millennia. Humans follow a cycle during the day that responds to environmental and internal changes. All living things have cycles that determine the natural processes that are essential for their existence. Flowers open in the morning and close in the evening, for example. Bears hibernate during winter and hunt in the spring.

Throughout the day, our activities occur cyclically, and this includes our appetite, our energy levels, our sleep or wakefulness patterns, and even our libido. Sleep is tied to these circadian rhythms that are determined by our biological clocks that are a series of proteins that act on the organs and tissues that make up our bodies, and these clocks work according to a master clock, located in the brain. For humans, this clock is part of the brain and is known as the suprachiasmatic nucleus, located in the hypothalamus. This is a neurological structure that relies on natural factors, such as genetics, which determine the circadian rhythm of our bodies, however, the master clock and, thus, the biological clocks are susceptible to environmental factors, and exposure to light, in particular (NIH, 2021, *Circadian Rhythms*).

Circadian rhythms influence when certain hormones are released, how alert we are at a given point during the day, when we get hungry, how our digestion works, and changes in our body temperature. But one of the most obvious functions of circadian rhythms is sleep regulation.

Our sleep is regulated through a hormone called melatonin. It makes us feel sleepy. Without melatonin, we might have a hard time falling asleep.

The release of melatonin is associated with exposure to light and is tied to the levels of light in the environment that we perceive. The brain receives information through the optic nerves and produces melatonin in low-light environments. It inhibits melatonin if there is too much light, because this suggests to the body that it's the day.

Most people's circadian rhythms are oriented around the fact that we mostly need to be active during the day and asleep during the night. When we experience, however, there are other factors that can impact our circadian rhythms.

One of the biggest sleep disruptors today is artificial light. Light bulbs, yes, but computer screens, TVs, smartphones, etc. can also inhibit the release of melatonin. Using these devices at night or having bright light before going to bed can make falling asleep more difficult and even make alterations to our circadian rhythms in a way that can hurt our health.

If you have ever traveled to another time zone, you probably saw the effects of a disruption of our circadian rhythm firsthand. Jet lag is another issue that can make our bodies feel confused, and it also leads to us feeling fatigued, struggling to think straight, and feeling drowsy all day long. Jet lag usually passes quickly enough, though, while other circadian cycle disruptions can have worse effects.

For example, shift work leads to sleep displacement and can contribute to significant negative health effects over time due to the disruption it causes to our natural circadian cycles. Working nights can lead a person to needing to stay awake and alert while their body requires sleep, which leads to health issues even if people can sleep for hours during the day (James, Honn, Gaddameedhi, & Van Dongen, 2017, *Shift Work: Disrupted Circadian Rhythms and Sleep-Implications for Health and Well-Being*).

It's best for our bodies when our sleep patterns align with our circadian rhythms at least most of the time. This means that we should recognize how these cycles work and see the 24-hour clock our body is running on.

Measuring and monitoring sleep

Though every member of the human species tends to follow the same life patterns and rhythms, there are many individual differences, and individuals can vary across their lifespans, too. Scientists have different ways of measuring your circadian rhythm, but these tend to be complex. Your sleep patterns can be easier to monitor, but it's important to remember that they are impacted by caffeine consumption, light exposure, stress, and other factors, especially sleep debt—the accumulated need for sleep that builds up when you can't get enough sleep for several nights. Consequently, many people believe they are not "morning people" when in fact they have been sleep-deprived for years, for example.

You can write down simple observations. Note when you get sleepy most days and write down your observations. Focus on when you seem to feel sleepy on a regular day and whether this time is when you tend to go to sleep. Consider how stable your sleep schedule is or whether it varies most days by more than an hour.

Pay attention to the time you usually wake up, especially without an alarm clock. If you are sleep-deprived, you might feel inclined to sleep in, of course, but what about the days when you got a mostly good night of rest? You can also track the times of day when you have the most energy and those when your energy dips.

There is now much debate around the concept of "chronotypes" which are individual biological variations on circadian rhythms. For example, you may be one of those people who genuinely does function best when working late at night and waking at around 11 in the morning. Even though these variations and types do exist, the fact is that the vast majority of people thrive on around 8 hours of sleep that falls at night. It can be difficult to decide at first what counts as your own natural tendency versus plain old bad habits, but be patient, and stay open-minded and aware of how you feel hour by hour.

In addition to your daytime observations, there are tools to help you track your sleep. Sleep apps can use different measures to track how much deep sleep you are getting. All you need is to place your phone on the mattress, and it will track how you are moving during the night. Fitness trackers, smart watches, and other wearables can also track sleep efficiency. While these trackers and apps are not perfect, they can provide valuable insights, especially if they detect that you are not getting enough deep sleep. Try to use other solutions, especially focusing on your own experiences and observations (Choi et al., 2018, *Smartphone Applications to Support Sleep Self-Management: Review and Evaluation*).

What information are you gathering here and why? You might notice the times when you feel drowsier or more alert. It's best to try to match your bedtime to the time when your body feels more tired and inclined to sleep, and wake up as close to the time when your internal clock is ready to go. This is not always easy to accomplish, but it can make a huge difference in how you feel and how much rest you get.

If you get information about sleep quality, you might rest better when following a particular schedule. Perhaps you get more deep sleep if you can manage to get to bed before midnight and less when you go to sleep after 2 a.m. All this can help you align your sleep schedule. Monitor your sleep for several days and nights, especially if you are faced with many factors that can be changing when you feel sleepy or energetic.

Schedule your sleep

This solution is not very glamorous but it gets the job done. By following a sleep schedule, you get your body accustomed to a specific rhythm that can align with your circadian rhythm closely and allow you to wake up rested and full of energy every day.

Of course, there are emergencies and other situations, but we should work to make a habit out of a regular sleep schedule and not disrupt it unless it's necessary. When you make it a priority, you can get better results that are certain to improve your health, well-being, and performance across the board. Isn't that worth adopting this structure?

Find a schedule that works for you. If you are used to going to bed late at night, it's pretty challenging to suddenly flip the script. You can work back toward an hour that feels comfortable. Move your sleep schedule by 15 minutes every day and adjust the wake-up time accordingly. Once you are at a good hour, make a habit of going to bed at this time. It might be hard at first, but soon it will become a lot easier, as your body learns to produce melatonin at the exact hour and allows you to fall asleep quickly, getting a better rest every night.

A sleep schedule is one of the central strategies you need to implement. In the following sections, we will look at other changes that can improve sleep quality.

Summary

- There is no area of life that isn't improved by a better sleep routine, and its importance extends to physical and psychological health, longevity, good immune function and creativity, to name a few.
- Sleep is influenced by a host of complex factors, including genetics, age, habit, season, and individual tendency and preference. Biohacking in this area may be nothing more than dropping lifelong bad habits around sleep and giving your body a proper chance at rejuvenation every evening!
- Without sleep, our moods, cognition, memory, and overall vitality take a knock. We not only think better when properly slept, but we are better able to regulate our emotions and learn faster.
- The circadian rhythm is the natural, inbuilt "biological clock" that runs on a 24-hour wake/sleep cycle. Because this rhythm influences hormone production and release, it impacts every system and organ of the body. Working

with and supporting our circadian rhythm is the key to optimal sleep health.

- One of the best and most impactful changes you can make to your health is to get into a regular sleep routine. This means waking and sleeping at the same time every day. Pay attention to your natural rhythms (possibly using an app to monitor) and then schedule a routine accordingly. Avoid sleeping in on weekends—when it comes to sleep, consistency really is the key.

CHAPTER 6

Sleep Like a Log

A good environment is essential for an equally good night's rest. Take a look at your bedroom and consider the changes that can help you sleep. After this, we will take a brief look at lifestyle changes, but for now, we will focus on the environment.

We sleep best when the room is dark, cool, well-ventilated, comfortable, and is a place used for sleeping.

Light and dark

We know that sleep is closely tied to the hormone melatonin, and that the production of melatonin is tied to light. When our optic nerves are sending light signals to the brain, it suggests that it's still daytime and we need to stay awake. Light can interfere with melatonin production, especially bright light bulbs, daylight, and the blue light that comes from our computer or phone screens. It confuses our bodies' internal clocks (Walker, 2018, *Why We Sleep*).

What can you do about it? The first trick is to make your bedroom as dark as possible. Try to get rid of light sources, even if they are tiny, as they might be disruptive. Blackout curtains are great, but if not, a mask to cover your eyes will also get rid of any undesirable light sources.

Try to dim the lights around you in the hour before going to bed. Stay away from blue light sources: if you must use your phone or laptop, you can install a blue light filter app or program that sometimes comes included with the device. This will make it easier to fall asleep after putting your gadget aside.

Temperature

We sleep better in colder rooms. Try to lower the temperature and make sure the room is ventilated. It's better to have a warm cover and pajamas than to have the room be warm. Find a cozy temperature for you and do what you can to fight the heat. Stuffy and hot rooms make for a poor night's rest.

Gadgets and tech

As mentioned above, try to keep your gadgets far away come bedtime or, at least, install programs that will reduce the light exposure. In general, having sources of entertainment and distraction can keep you up longer. You have probably stayed up scrolling through Facebook or looking at endless lists of 20 hilarious cat pictures. The problem here is that our willpower might be depleted, and we might find it harder to stop scrolling and put the phone away (Kamphorst, Nauts, De Ridder, & Anderson, 2018, *Too Depleted to Turn In: The Relevance of End-of-the-Day Resource Depletion for Reducing Bedtime Procrastination*). It's better to implement solutions that support good and healthy choices, like installing apps that will remind you to go to bed or shut off the connection, so that you don't have to rely on your tired self to make the choice.

For some people, the idea is not appealing. They only feel they get a chance to relax before bed. If that's your case, try to schedule free time before it. Look for other spaces in your day when you can relax without making sleep any less of a priority.

Apps and programs can shut off your internet connection or turn off your device automatically to make it harder to keep scrolling. If you feel that it's an important part of your day, try to be aware of the choices you are making.

It's useful to build bedtime habits that do not involve technology and get a break from all the stimulation it involves. Reading and other relaxing activities can help you fall asleep easier, unless you are the type to get swept up in the book, of course.

Watch out for apps with infinite scrolling, like TikTok, Instagram, and Facebook, where you can continue to browse content without a stopping point. Don't let these apps deprive you of sleep.

Keep these things OUT of your bedroom

The strictest sleep researchers suggest that you should try to use your bedroom, or at least your bed, only for sleeping or almost exclusively for sleeping (Walker, 2018, *Why We Sleep*). This is not always possible, but it's a good idea to try and avoid watching films or eating in bed. It helps you train your brain to associate the bed with sleeping.

If you can manage it, it's a good idea to have your devices outside the bedroom, or at least beyond your reach from the bed. Place them so that the temptation is a little further away. Don't keep your TV in the bedroom either and minimize the distractions.

We have mentioned the importance of darkness for rest, so it's a good idea to move everything that blinks or emits light away. Avoid noise-making appliances, too.

If you can separate your spaces for rest and work, it's a good idea to have a separate office. Not everyone can have a workspace within the house, but if you need it, move it away from the bed and adapt a desk or another part of the bedroom. Keep your work away from your bed, too, to avoid thinking about it or stressing about it. Make your bedroom a space of pure relaxation.

It's a good idea to bring in stuff that helps you relax, like candles, pillows, a book to read, water, and more. A comfy, cozy bedroom is better for your rest, and it should be a place where you feel comfortable. Depending on your preferences, keep it minimalist or have objects that are pleasant and associated with good emotions.

A controversial topic is whether you sleep better alone or with a partner. There is mixed evidence, so consider when you feel more rested (Richter et al., 2018, *Two in a Bed: The Influence of Couple Sleeping and Chronotypes on Relationship and Sleep. An Overview*). Some couples opt to sleep apart due to their differing needs and find that it strongly improves sleep quality, while others enjoy the togetherness more. It's worth addressing sleeping with your partner and see what works best to ensure you both get a good night's sleep. Don't be afraid to set boundaries.

So, to recap:

Keep your bedroom dark during the night. Avoid even small light sources. Try to catch natural light or bright light in the mornings and during the day, but avoid it before sleep. Dim the lights before going to bed. Avoid gadgets before bedtime. If you can't or don't want to, then use blue light filters. Keep the room cool and free of distractions. Set boundaries with your partner to ensure you are both well-rested.

The importance of daylight

For most of human history, our circadian rhythms were guided by daylight. Like animals and plants, we moved according to the day-night cycle, going to sleep when it was dark and waking when it was light. However, artificial light has changed that. If we want, we can have a never-ending day, at least as far as our bodies are concerned.

Even though artificial light has been around for a while, our bodies still use light as the signal for determining whether it is time to be awake or time to be asleep. The information about light comes in through the eyes, mainly, and our body calibrates hormone and neurotransmitter production depending on this data. Exposing yourself to sunlight in the morning and during the day is a good solution for improving your sleep during the night (Figueiro et al., 2017, *The Impact of Daytime Light Exposures on Sleep and Mood in Office Workers*).

Light exposure in the morning and during the day helps our body regulate serotonin levels during the day and improve melatonin production during the night. We need daylight to help our hormone production stay aligned with the natural cycle of the body. Serotonin production occurs throughout the day and drops in the evening, when our bodies release melatonin. Serotonin is also associated with adequate melatonin production. This means that sunlight is connected to sleep quality at night (Figueiro et al., 2017, *The Impact of Daytime Light Exposures on Sleep and Mood in Office Workers*).

Cortisol is another hormone that can interfere with sleep when it appears outside of the body's natural cycle. We need to have peak cortisol levels in the morning, but not in the evening, which is also regulated by sunlight exposure.

What are the practical implications of this? It means that we need to increase sunlight exposure during the morning and during the day. When you wake up, try to get sunlight as quickly as you can. Walk outside during the day and get sunlight exposure. Make sure your eyes are exposed to the light—watch out for filters, sunglasses, or any other type of eyewear that can filter the light. Allow the light to hit your face and get some sun, in the morning and during the day.

What happens if it's cloudy outside? It doesn't matter—the sunlight is still there, so you should try to get some exposure even if the day is not looking bright. Light comes through the clouds, even if it doesn't feel like it.

Some people have a harder situation, however. If you live in a place where daylight is lacking, especially during the winter days, when it sets soon, you might find yourself leaving your home in the darkness and coming back after work in the darkness, too. What can you do then? If you can, leave your workplace during lunch to get some sun. If it's not possible or not enough, you can look into other options. There are special lamps and boxes that are used for treating seasonal depression (tied to a lack of sunlight, too) that simulate daylight.

Get light in the morning and during the day! It will help you sleep better at night.

Lifestyle changes

Environmental changes can help your sleep schedule stick and ensure that nothing is standing between you and a good night's sleep. But sometimes it's useful to add some lifestyle changes, especially if you find that some factors, like caffeine or alcohol, have a strong effect on your sleep quality.

Diet and supplements

Some foods seem to have an effect on sleep quality. Foods like cherries, milk, kiwi, fatty fish, and other foods promote better quality even when eaten during the day, but the findings for this are still preliminary (St-Onge, Mitic, & Pietrolungo, 2016, *Effects of Diet on Sleep Quality*).

The effects of sleep disruptors are a bit better outlined. Caffeine and drinks that contain it—in particular, coffee, black tea, and chocolate—can influence sleep for 12 hours after consumption. It's recommended that you avoid coffee at least 6 hours before bed and do not take it after noon if you struggle to fall asleep. Alcohol can make people sleepy, but in reality, it disrupts our natural sleep cycle, so it's not a good idea to take it as an aid for falling asleep.

Some supplements are presented as sleeping aids, but many do not have any evidence. Omega-3, just like fatty fish, could help, but it's important to be critical of aids that make big promises. With regards to medication for sleeping, in particular, it's important not to take anything without supervision from a doctor, even things sold over the counter like melatonin. Some of these medications can have unexpected results in the long term.

Some dietary changes can improve your sleep, but they are a supporting change, not a main change. Watch out for supplements and medications, and take them with caution and under supervision.

Exercise

Exercise during the day can help you improve sleep at night. Increasing activity during the day can help people sleep better at night, and exercise has even been proposed as a potential treatment avenue for sleep disturbances. Sleep and exercise have a two-way relationship, as exercise can improve sleep and sleep can make it easier for people to stay active (Kline, 2014, *The Bidirectional Relationship Between Exercise and Sleep: Implications for Exercise Adherence and Sleep Improvement*). To reap the most benefits, however, schedule your exercise sessions for mornings and earlier in the day. Avoid exercise for three hours before bedtime, as it can interfere with your sleep.

Stress and relaxation

Stress can interfere with sleep as well, reducing deep sleep and REM sleep, which are the ones that provide us with the most rest and benefits (Kim & Dimsdale, 2007, *The Effect of Psychosocial Stress on Sleep: A Review of Polysomnographic Evidence*).

Reducing stress and practicing things like meditation or relaxation can also improve our sleep quality.

Try to practice things that relax you before bed: reading, a hot bath, a quiet hobby, drawing, journaling, etc. Don't lie in bed worrying about things. If you can't sleep, get up and do something quiet. You can go back to bed once you feel drowsy.

Naps

Naps are another contentious issue. They seem to have significant benefits for our mood and cognitive ability for people who did not experience problems with their sleep and might be advantageous on days when the person has not rested well (Milnet & Cote, 2009, *Benefits of Napping in Healthy Adults: Impact of Nap Length, Time of Day, Age, and Experience with Napping*). People who are implementing a sleep schedule for the first time or are having difficulties falling asleep at night, though, should probably steer clear of naps in the daytime.

Naps can interfere with falling asleep at night. If you struggle with it or are trying to stick to your schedule, it's better to stay awake during the day rather than nap. If you have a strong sleep schedule, however, naps can be enjoyable and helpful tools for those days when you did not manage to get enough rest.

Creating a wind-down routine

Any parent will tell you that a bedtime routine is important for any kid to get them to wind down and go to sleep without protest. But this kind of routine can be great for adults and help you improve your sleep quality.

You can create your own routine before bed, which has several advantages. It's likely to make it easier for you to fall asleep and also allows you to maintain a stable sleep quality every day, as a ritual that leads up to going to bed helps you wind down at the same time each night.

The nighttime routine can start with some relaxing activities. You should avoid anything that is too high on action and focus on calmer stuff, like reading, meditating, journaling or writing, or talking to family. Find the activities that relax you the most and leave you feeling calm and ready to sleep. There are hundreds of apps and resources that are meant to help you wind down, such as apps that offer relaxing stories or meditations or music, nature sounds and white noise, and more. You can look for podcasts, playlists, and apps that are meant to help you sleep better.

A hot shower is a wonderful activity to try before bed, as it's quite relaxing and also helps your body cool down, which makes falling asleep easier.

Make sure to dim the lights in the evening. Another good strategy before bed is to write down every thought that could keep you up. When you put them down on paper, it becomes easier to disconnect from your ideas, especially if you are prone to worry.

Some small hacks can make a difference in the environment. Open the window to ventilate the room, for example, and set out your pillows and pajamas. You can use a mask for sleeping to increase the quality of your rest if you can't get blackout curtains. Putting on the mask is a good way of cutting yourself off from the waking world and getting all ready to snooze.

Some days, sleep just won't come. That's okay. Don't stress too much about it and try to avoid situations where you toss and turn for hours. Instead, if you have been in bed for a while, get up and go back to a relaxing activity of your choice with dim lights until you're sleepy.

Having an established bedtime ritual can help your body prepare for sleep and start releasing the necessary hormones, like melatonin.

Rituals build up the habit of going to bed at the same time each night, and if you can repeat it every day of the week, you are less likely to stay up watching shows or procrastinating going to bed.

Add a wake-up routine

In the morning, all our best intentions to maintain a sleep schedule can go out of the window if we are not careful. A good way to counteract the desire to snooze for a few minutes that can turn into much longer periods of time is to establish a pleasant and effective morning routine.

The morning routine serves the same function as the bedtime routine; it just prepares your body for the day and allows you to make a habit of maintaining a regular sleep schedule, even on the days where you don't have to go to work.

A morning routine can benefit, first, from a lot of light. Natural light exposure can wake up your body. If you can't look at natural light, simply turning on the lamps in your home can do the trick. Make sure you get a lot of light when you wake up, as it helps you stay awake.

A good idea is to have a pleasant activity scheduled for the morning. Whether it's exercise, meditation, a delicious breakfast, or some time spent reading or writing or creating, a fun activity can motivate you to get out of bed.

A shower with hot and cold water can also help you wake up and feel ready. You might try breathing exercises, meditation, and short, easy workouts that get the blood flowing.

Mornings can be hard. If you wake up and always feel tired, like you did not sleep, you are likely not getting enough rest, or there is something affecting the quality of your sleep, especially if you do get your 8 hours and still feel sluggish the next day. A ritual can help you push your body into wakefulness in a more gentle and pleasant manner and ensure your biological clock is aware that it is the morning and time to be alert and ready to start the day.

If you rise early, it's easier to go to sleep at night. While you should not push yourself to always rise at an uncomfortably early time, try to find the best hour for you to wake and keep this schedule as much as the one for going to bed.

When you are biohacking your sleep, it's best to keep to true and tried methods, even if they are less exciting than promises of overhauling your need for sleep. As the importance of rest for your body is so significant, messing with it should be done with care, as problems like insomnia can be not only unpleasant to experience but also outright dangerous. In this final section, we will take a look at the myths and ideas about sleep to stay away from.

Can you sleep four hours a day or less?

No. Most adults, with a few exceptional winners of the genetic sleep lottery, require at least 7 hours a night, and some need even more. There is a prevalent myth, however, making the rounds online that you can train your body to get by on just four hours of sleep, or even change your schedule and fit these hours through the day and the night.

What we know about sleep is not consistent with this idea. You cannot change your body's need for sleep; the only way is to try and improve sleep quality. Getting only four hours of sleep is harmful and does not change the need for sleep. It does have all the negative effects we have discussed, though, and can lead to significant health problems. If you need more sleep, you can't teach yourself to need less.

Remember that it is possible to get used to the effects of sleep deprivation and treat it as normal, however, this doesn't mean that this is a good idea in the long run. While life makes a strict schedule difficult sometimes, trying to find a schedule that works for you is a better solution.

Can I make up for my sleep debt by napping?

A nap can help with feeling sleep-deprived, but breaking down sleep doesn't work as a long-term strategy. Our sleep is cyclical, and our bodies need time to experience each cycle. It's better to try and get as much sleep as we can at night. Naps can be helpful but are not a solution to sleep deprivation that occurs regularly. In general, it is suggested that the best naps last between 15 and 45 minutes, in order to make sure you wake up feeling refreshed and not sluggish.

Can I sleep in on weekends to make up for my sleep debt?

If you are rarely sleep-deprived, you can sleep in on the weekends. But generally, it's not an effective long-term strategy. You can't make up for a week of bad sleep by getting more hours on a single day. It's also a good idea to try and keep a schedule every day, even on the weekends, as changing the time you go to sleep and wake up can really mess with your biological clock and circadian rhythms.

Sleeping pills

Sleeping pills have many useful functions. Under medical supervision, they can help you normalize your sleep schedule, get through a tough time, or improve symptoms and problems like insomnia. Sleeping pills, however, are not a catch-all solution, for several reasons.

Some types of pills, when used without moderation, can make it difficult for the person to fall asleep without them. Other types can produce residual effects, like cognitive impairment, lack of coordination, dizziness, and more, interfering with daily life (Fitzgerald & Vietri, 2015, *Residual Effects of Sleep Medications are Commonly Reported and Associated with Impaired Patient-Reported Outcomes Among Insomnia Patients in the United States*). Sleeping pills, even over-the-counter remedies like melatonin, should be employed with care and with the help and supervision of a professional to ensure the negative effects are minimal.

In some cases, the pills are important and useful. But non-medication strategies can be more sustainable and have fewer side effects.

Disproven hacks

There are also some tips and ideas that get circulated widely or shared as common knowledge, while they are not true. It can be a bad idea to employ myths in the pursuit of a better night's rest.

A common and false idea is that alcohol helps you rest. While it can make you sleepy, it inhibits deep and restorative sleep, leaving you tired the next day.

Another myth is the idea that eight hours a day is all that matters. First, it seems that we need those hours to follow each other; a daytime nap can't make up for our nightly deficits. Additionally, we do not rest as well during the day, and it seems that our body suffers when it has to be up and awake at night, as shown by the problems faced by shift workers. Sleeping at night or mostly at night helps us stay in line with our body's circadian rhythms. You can't make up for lost sleep by napping or making it up during the day. You also can't train yourself not to sleep throughout the night (Robbins et al., 2019, *Sleep Myths: an Expert-led Study to Identify False Beliefs About Sleep that Impinge Upon Population Sleep Health Practices*).

Sleeping in on the weekends is another failed strategy for getting your sleep back on track. While it can be hard to implement, experts recommend maintaining a regular schedule throughout the week rather than sleeping in (Robbins et al., 2019, *Sleep Myths: An Expert-Led Study to Identify False Beliefs About Sleep that Impinge Upon Population Sleep Health Practices*).

It's worth noting also that many of the tricks we use to stay awake when tired are not that effective. This is something to keep in mind if you have to drive, especially. Cold water, fresh air, or a turned-up radio won't help you all that much and won't prevent microsleep, which is the real danger of driving under the influence of a few sleepless nights.

Another common problem is the snooze button. It can feel satisfying to hit it and go back to sleep, but that's worse than allowing ourselves to simply sleep in longer rather than break the rest into fragments, as this makes the situation worse.

Overall, be wary of "revolutionary" sleep hacks, as they might harm your sleep schedule more than they fix it. Biohacking through establishing bedtimes and wake-up times, exercise, environmental changes, and so on is less thrilling, of course, but it also ensures that we get the results we want without compromising our health in the process.

Understanding why and how sleep works can help us understand why we can't get by on four hours a night, or why our bodies really can't be trained to thrive on less sleep. While hustle culture and societal demands might eschew sleep in favor of productivity and other pursuits, the reality is that prioritizing things other than our rest is likely to end up hurting us physically and emotionally and compromise our ability to get other things done—especially done well.

Living in a state of chronic sleep deprivation is not only harmful, but also actively unpleasant and difficult, even if we accept it as part of the routine. Sleep changes everything and improves our lives in unexpected ways, acting across the boards with a myriad of positive effects.

Summary

- There are plenty of ways to improve a less-than-optimal sleep routine.
- Environmental changes include working with your body's natural light-driven rhythm; i.e., exposure to natural light upon waking, and avoidance of artificial light to extend or interfere with the normal circadian rhythm. An ideal sleeping environment is also the right temperature, and relatively free of noisy or bright gadgets that can disturb sleep or can be sources of stress or distraction.
- Don't do anything in your bed except sleep, to help your brain form the right associations. Don't watch TV, work, or browse social media in your bed; if you can't sleep, get out of bed so you don't associate sleeplessness with that environment.
- Lifestyle changes include making diet and exercise changes conducive to good sleep; for example, avoiding coffee, alcohol, or strenuous workouts too close to bedtime. Practice relaxation techniques throughout the day but consider having a daily "wind-down" routine

before bed, too. For that matter, a wake-up routine can also be a healthy daily ritual. Naps can be okay, but they don't work for everyone. Avoid them if they impair your normal sleep schedule.

- Educate yourself about sleep health, and forget popular myths, such as the idea that you can function on four hours of sleep with no ill effect. Though there are individual differences, the vast majority of people need around 7 to 8 hours. You cannot make up for a "sleep debt" with a nap or extra sleep on the weekends—instead, get back into your healthy routine again ASAP. The remedy is always to get straight back into routine, rather than "catching up".
- Sleeping pills can be an occasional and temporary solution, but are best avoided since they have many negative, residual effects. Most sleep hacks are harmful in the long run; instead, the best strategy is a rock-solid routine.

Summary Guide

Chapter 1: Take Back Your Focus

- Dopamine is a powerful and complex neurotransmitter, but the modern world can play havoc with its healthy and optimal balance. Dopamine allows us to feel pleasure and reward, experience anticipation and desire, and seek out novelty. A dysregulated dopamine system can result in significant impairment to our motivation, our ability to experience pleasure, impulse control, mood, concentration, attention, self-discipline, and desire, among other things.
- We are not at the mercy of our neurochemistry, however—the brain is plastic and can be changed if we are aware of its mechanisms and work to support it strategically.
- Part of what makes behavioral change so hard can be thought of as dopamine addiction, and consequently a "dopamine detox" can help

bring more regulation to the way we process information and act in each moment.

- If dopamine is a biochemical proxy for willpower, then learning to biohack it allows us to cultivate more self-control, self-awareness, and self-regulation. We can use different techniques and methods to help improve our behavior, via the dopamine system.
- We can create an environment that is supportive of focus and attention; for example, by removing distractions like smartphones. Use apps or programs to moderate your behavior or enlist the help of others to keep you accountable to your goals.
- Lapses are inevitable, so practice compassion rather than beating yourself up. Learn from your mistakes and move on, rather than dwelling on them. Likewise, think small and don't bite off more than you can chew. Some techniques will work for you, some not. Experiment a little.

Chapter 2: A Detox To End Them All

- Though dopamine is a natural part of the brain's chemistry, excessive levels can mimic addiction profiles, and hence a dopamine detox can help reset our brain to optimal levels, and allow us to experience challenge, reward and novelty in new, healthier ways.

- Detoxing involves reducing “easy” tasks that provide bursts of low-effort dopamine (such as social media, sugar, alcohol, shopping, or pornography) and replacing them with activities such as meditating, exercise, fasting, hobbies, reading, or sports.
- Feeling bored, deprived, frustrated, or even angry during a detox is normal, and a sign of how necessary a purge is! Persist with discomfort, however, and you will gradually recalibrate yourself. In time, you will train your brain to enjoy productive, healthy and gradual pleasures and accomplishments rather than instant gratification and distraction.
- Choose a 1-, 3-, or 7-day detox according to your needs, and work to rewire your brain and consider which behaviors you want to keep in your life, and which are harmful. By dialing down the thrills and instant gratification, you allow yourself the chance to think more deeply about your more authentic values and desires in life.
- A 7-day detox can be powerful, but needs some strategic planning ahead of time. Factor in plenty of opportunities for mindfulness and reflection, work with your boredom by anticipating it and choosing not to resist it, and focus on the process of what is happening with your cravings and your denial of those cravings.
- Good sleep habits, nutrition, and exercise are part and parcel of rewiring your brain. Liberally

use awareness and relaxation techniques. The goal is not deprivation, but to rework your relationship to pleasure, action, and awareness. The goal is to gain conscious mastery and control over your own life and what you most want to create for yourself.

Chapter 3: Fuel for Life

- Though nutrition science is always advancing and changing, we do know that good food is essential for a good life, and that the ideal human diet broadly follows Michael Pollan's nutrition rule: "Eat real food. Not too much. Mostly plants."
- Flexibility is key: rigid rules are unsustainable.
- There are countless diet philosophies out there; for example, the Mediterranean diet (plant-based and low meat, but heavily featuring olive oil and moderation) the Okinawan diet (lean seafood protein, starchy plants, and good fats), and the keto diet (emphasis on low carb, high protein, and high fat eating that induces ketogenesis in the body).
- No single food is a miracle cure, but there are certain "superfoods" that are especially nutritious, such as broccoli or blueberries.
- Supplements, too, can boost a diet, although not all supplements are created equal, and no supplement is a replacement for a healthy diet. Since supplements are not FDA regulated, it's

up to you to do your research. It's best to tailor your supplement use to fit your unique diet and lifestyle.

- There is increasing evidence for the beneficial use of probiotics and prebiotics (which is essentially the fiber that probiotics feed on).
- Probiotics can correct imbalances in the body's all-important gut microbiome, the health of which has far-reaching effects on every part of your body, including your weight and overall mental health. Though available in supplement form, it's best to get probiotic cultures into your diet naturally, with fermented foods such as kefir, yogurt, or kimchi. In addition, plenty of plant fiber and a diet low in sugar and alcohol will support a healthy gut bacterial balance.

Chapter 4: Nudging Your Nutrition

- Though we all know the principles of a healthy diet, cultivating good habits takes time and effort.
- "Nudge theory" is all about the small changes we can make to our environment that will prompt the desired behavior. Everything is a choice, but we can make the right choice easier and more automatic by tweaking the environment.
- Ensure that there is always a feedback mechanism in place for any behavior, and try to simplify complex behaviors and choices as much as possible. Examples of nudges include

keeping snack foods in the house, avoiding tempting aisles in the grocery store, or connecting exercise to other, more established habits in your routine. Done right, a nudge helps you do the right thing without expending too much extra willpower!

- Caroline Arnold's concept of micro-resolutions tells us that big things are possible when we commit to tiny steps. If you make a small but specific change in the right direction and *stick to it*, the cumulative effect can be immense.
- To make a micro-resolution, identify a target behavior, then make tiny commitments toward change, avoiding anything dramatic or extreme. Think small but think strategically—make the smallest change you know you can stick with indefinitely.
- Two factors we know influence our eating behavior are light and temperature. Working with our biological rhythms is easier than working against them, and is more likely to lead to sustainable and healthful changes.
- At the bare minimum, expose yourself to natural light on waking in the morning, and avoid artificial light late into the night. Similarly, heat and cold can be used to wake the body up or encourage the natural signals to sleep.

Chapter 5: The True Importance of Sleep

- There is no area of life that isn't improved by a better sleep routine, and its importance extends to physical and psychological health, longevity, good immune function and creativity, to name a few.

- Sleep is influenced by a host of complex factors, including genetics, age, habit, season, and individual tendency and preference. Biohacking in this area may be nothing more than dropping lifelong bad habits around sleep and giving your body a proper chance at rejuvenation every evening!
- Without sleep, our moods, cognition, memory, and overall vitality take a knock. We not only think better when properly slept, but we are better able to regulate our emotions and learn faster.
- The circadian rhythm is the natural, inbuilt "biological clock" that runs on a 24-hour wake/sleep cycle. Because this rhythm influences hormone production and release, it impacts every system and organ of the body. Working with and supporting our circadian rhythm is the key to optimal sleep health.
- One of the best and most impactful changes you can make to your health is to get into a regular sleep routine. This means waking and sleeping at the same time every day. Pay attention to your natural rhythms (possibly using an app to monitor) and then schedule a routine accordingly. Avoid sleeping in on weekends—when it comes to sleep, consistency really is the key.

Chapter 6: Sleep Like a Log

- There are plenty of ways to improve a less-than-optimal sleep routine.
- Environmental changes include working with your body's natural light-driven rhythm; i.e., exposure to natural light upon waking, and avoidance of artificial light to extend or interfere with the normal circadian rhythm. An ideal sleeping environment is also the right temperature, and relatively free of noisy or bright gadgets that can disturb sleep or can be sources of stress or distraction.
- Don't do anything in your bed except sleep, to help your brain form the right associations. Don't watch TV, work, or browse social media in your bed; if you can't sleep, get out of bed so you don't associate sleeplessness with that environment.
- Lifestyle changes include making diet and exercise changes conducive to good sleep; for example, avoiding coffee, alcohol, or strenuous workouts too close to bedtime. Practice relaxation techniques throughout the day but consider having a daily "wind-down" routine before bed, too. For that matter, a wake-up routine can also be a healthy daily ritual. Naps can be okay, but they don't work for everyone. Avoid them if they impair your normal sleep schedule.

- Educate yourself about sleep health, and forget popular myths, such as the idea that you can function on four hours of sleep with no ill effect. Though there are individual differences, the vast majority of people need around 7 to 8 hours. You cannot make up for a "sleep debt" with a nap or extra sleep on the weekends—instead, get back into your healthy routine again ASAP. The remedy is always to get straight back into routine, rather than "catching up".
- Sleeping pills can be an occasional and temporary solution, but are best avoided since they have many negative, residual effects. Most sleep hacks are harmful in the long run; instead, the best strategy is a rock-solid routine.

About the Author

Nick Trenton grew up as a farm boy in rural Illinois in USA.

He obtained a BS in Economics, followed by an MA in Behavioural Psychology.

Nick likes to say that he has become a professional expert at one of his favourite hobbies: people-watching. He is an accomplished skier and dreams of travelling the world and hosting a food show like Anthony Bourdain.

He currently lives in Chicago, USA.

Other titles by Nick Trenton,
published by Manjul/Amaryllis